JavaScript Inheritance and Object Programming

JSW: JSWindows, v2

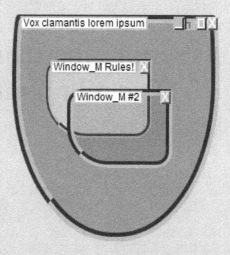

JavaScript Inheritance and Object Programming

Martin Rinehart

All text, code and illustrations by Martin Rinehart, a full-time frontend engineer. He can be contacted through http://www.martinrinehart.com/.

Many thanks to Technical Editors Robert Franzese, founder of Zen40.com, Eric Schmidt of Microsoft Corporation and Assaf Shemesh, an expert in software development and management. Without their efforts this book would have many more errors.

Dedicated to Brendan Eich, who wrote JavaScript and gave us object programming.

JavaScript Inheritance and Object Programming

A Note for the Implementers

JavaScript, or more exactly, the subset of JavaScript Crockford identifies as "The Good Parts," is a beautiful language. It is small, yet expressive. It's combination of C with functional programming and object programming gives it extraordinary depth. In nearly a half century of programming I have used dozens of languages. Only two of them, JavaScript is one, have been languages I've loved.

Today there are people working to free JavaScript from the browser, to further empower JavaScript (FileWriter and WebGL, to mention personal favorites) and to bring it up to professional speed. My apologies to the latter group. In many ways, object programming is the enemy of compiled speed.

So a word of encouragement and advice to our courageous implementers. First, making JavaScript run at some reasonable fraction of C's speed is a magnificent goal. More power to you! (And yes, that's self-serving. You are giving more power to all of us who write JavaScript. We love it and we thank you for it.)

Second, removing object programming to gain speed cuts out the heart to save the patient. Object programming is not your enemy, it is the essence of the language. Look on it as a challenge, as the Everest of your profession. The view from the top will be spectacular. Object programming at half the speed of C will be breathtaking.

Martin Rinehart, 8 June 2013
Hudson Valley, New York

Website

This book is the sixth "knowit" at the author's website, MartinRinehart.com. From the home page, click "Knowits" and then "JIOP".

The gateway page holds the notes (both footnotes and bibliography). Hyperlinks are online in the book (so the text of this book is uninterrupted, and so you can click on the references).

From the gateway page, sub menus link you to the "User Guide" to the *JSWindows* system, the engineer's reference material and the source code.

Introduction

Within the JavaScript community there is a great deal of misinformation regarding inheritance. Some comes from object-oriented programmers (C++ and its offspring like Java and C#) looking for, and not finding, their familiar classes. Some comes from JavaScript programmers looking for Self-style prototypal inheritance, which JavaScript's prototypes are not very good at.

In this small volume we begin at the beginning, discussing objects, their place in software and the benefits we expect from them. We continue to first define terms like "class" (three meanings) and "inheritance." With a common terminology we then look at how class-based and prototypal inheritance can be implemented in JavaScript. To leap ahead, we will propose ways in which JavaScript is best served by minimizing the long inheritance chains associated with object-oriented programming languages.

1

OOP inheritance is very different from prototypal inheritance. They are widely misunderstood as two ways of achieving the same result. Their similarities are more superficial than profound. We have to understand both to understand JavaScript's hybrid class/prototypal object model.

Throughout the book we look at our *JSWindows* sample system. These are windows, JavaScript style:

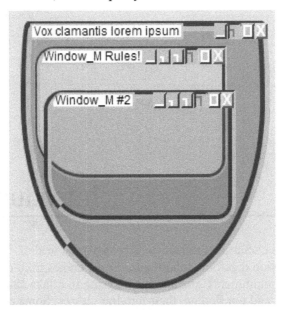

These windows can be dragged to new positions, resized, minimized, maximized and so on. They are programmed in JavaScript but with OOP inheritance.

JSWindows does not use prototypal inheritance. It's goal, in addition to being a working window system, was to demonstrate class-based inheritance in JavaScript without additional library code. It was intended to demonstrate the use of long inheritance chains without the use of JavaScript's prototype chain.

Along the way, we also examine JavaScript's object programming (OP) abilities, abilities that are the true distinction between class-based OOP and JavaScript's hybrid object model. *JSWindows* library code (not inheritance-related) makes extensive use of object programming. JavaScript programmers almost all use object programming, though many are not aware of its profound importance.

Last, we show how *JSWindows* uses "capabilities," a hybrid of Java's interfaces and JavaScript's mixins. We show that capabilities give us the benefits of inheritance without the problems associated with mapping complex real world relationships to OOP-limited models. (Java replaced multiple inheritance with interfaces, and we were big fans.) Object programming enables our capabilities.

Finally, we note that inheritance, specifically OOP inheritance, is a valuable tool for the advanced JavaScript programmer. (Prototypal inheritance may also be valuable, for those so inclined. If you understand that these are two different models, you can use both together.) Once you understand the importance of object programming, however, inheritance assumes a far less prominent part in your systems' architectures.

We make assertions about JavaScript's abilities along the way. The last two chapters may interest those who accept nothing without proof. The first discusses JavaScript's relationship to traditional OOP concepts, such as encapsulation and polymorphism. The second elaborates on the details of the JavaScript constructor mechanism.

1 Objects

Objects were a software experiment that worked. They began in research labs in the late 1970s. They became a new, mainstream programming paradigm in the 1980s. By the '90s, languages that were being created (Java, JavaScript, Python, Ruby) were all object-based. Languages that predated objects were being retrofitted. Today even 50-year old languages (Basic, Cobol, Fortran) have adopted objects.

In this book we will be examining two forms of inheritance and alternatives to inheritance. We need to understand the benefits of objects to see how these alternatives provide (or not) the benefits of programming with objects.

We will also be drawing examples from our *JSWindows* demonstration system. It is introduced at the end of this chapter.

Reasons for Objects

There are a lot of reasons to prefer programming with objects. We'll discuss three here.

Objects Do Methods

First, the syntax has things doing things just as happens outside of the world of software. The things objects do are small software programs, functions that the object can perform, commonly called methods. If you program a dog (object) to speak (method) you express it directly:

```
dog.speak(); // says "Woof, woof"
```

Many objects can implement the same action (method) with variations appropriate for each, as Listing 1-1 shows.

Listing 1-1

```
parrot.speak(); // "Polly want a cracker."
kitten.speak(); // "mew, mew"
```

If your parrots and kittens use different methods for speaking, object systems will choose the appropriate method for you. Chapter 8 explains *subtype polymorphism*, the principle underlying the selection of object-appropriate methods.

Event-Driven Programming

Second, few programs now do anything except by user direction. Most programs paint an interface (menus, icons, buttons) and wait for a user command. This is called "event-driven" programming. When the user clicks the "save" icon, the user's document is written to disk. Internally, the user action could trigger a very small program:

```
user_data.save();
```

Again, it uses the `noun.verb()` syntax. This brings us to the main reason for the success of objects.

Again, it uses the `noun.verb()` syntax. This brings us to the main reason for the success of objects.

Taming Exponential Complexity

As programs grow in size, complexity increases exponentially. We have all used systems that never seemed to be robust. Fixing this broke that. If the complexity is ever successfully tamed, it is after immense expense. Objects help shrink the size and limit the complexity. That reduces the effort (expense).

Let's think about a simple example. A small non-object program might require a thousand lines of code. The same job using objects might require ten methods, each only a hundred lines of code. The ten small methods will be far cheaper to write and vastly cheaper to debug.

As we look at *JSWindows'* code, you will see many features that take surprisingly little code and live comfortably outside of other parts of the system.

Class-Based v. Prototypal

Objects come in many guises. We will be using class-based object-oriented programming (OOP, based on classes) and JavaScript's hybrid class/prototypal object model.

Object systems go back to Simula and SmallTalk, in the late '70s. These found the mainstream when Bjarne Stroustrup, at Bell Labs, wrote a compiler that output programs in plain C from an object-enhanced form he called C++. (During the '80s, C was the dominant language for professional programming on non-IBM mainframes and almost all minicomputers and microcomputers.) C++ was first available in 1983. By the end of the decade it had become ubiquitous.

To add objects to C, Stroustrup made some sacrifices. His enhanced C used class modules (more on these shortly) that were not objects, but that defined objects. Despite protests from purists, Stroustrup's limited features were well chosen and programmers were delighted with its improvements over original C. Other languages, such as Java

(1995) adopted the C++ object model. Programming in C++ and its progeny is called "object-oriented programming" or "class-based" (aka "classical") OOP.

Class-based OOP relies on class software that defines the objects created. The programmer decides what features each group of objects will need and programs an appropriate class software module that will create objects with those features.

By contrast, the "prototypal" object paradigm does not use class modules. The programmer creates a prototype object and other objects are then cloned from the prototype. This was an experimental object model from Self, a language that evolved from SmallTalk.

JavaScript's original author, Brendan Eich, adopted the prototypal model, partially, in a scripting language for Netscape's then market-leading web browser, Netscape Navigator. JavaScript, born in 1995, combined class-based and prototypal forms. As JavaScript is, to date, the only language available for writing programs that run in all browsers, it has exploded in popularity as the web has exploded.

Class-based OOP and JavaScript perform similar functions and provide similar benefits.

Programmers have begun to discover that JavaScript supports almost complete object programming (defined in Chapter 3) and this is a major advance over the limitations of the class-based model, quite separate from and far more important than JavaScript's prototypal features.

So what are objects?

Objects Up Close

An object is a collection of properties (often a set, but "set" has a mathematical meaning we do not want here). Properties are named values. Values may be, depending on the language, simple values (boolean, integer, character), composite values built from other values (arrays, objects) or, in languages capable of functional programming, functions or other blocks of code. (JavaScript also implements functional programming borrowed from the Scheme language, a dialect of Lisp.)

Some authors use the word "property" to specifically mean what we call "data properties"—properties that are not methods. We find this misleading in a language where functions are first-class objects.

In JavaScript, property names must be strings. In most class-based OOP languages they must be strings that are limited by the restrictions imposed on variable names.

Objects also are permitted direct access to a collection of functions (commonly called "instance methods") that are part of the class software (in class-based languages) or the prototype (in JavaScript). These functions are separate from, but available to, the objects.

All dogs, in the example above, could access the `speak()` method:

```
dog.speak(); // says "Woof, woof"
```

Here, `speak()` is a property of dog objects. In the text, trailing parentheses indicate that the property is executable code, called a method. This is one of the two main categories of object properties.

Data Properties

Objects may have data properties. These are often said to describe an object's "state." A dog might have properties such as `name`, `breed` and `date-of-birth`. Each dog (called an "object instance" or, in class-based OOP, an "instance" of the dog class) will have space allocated to store each of these properties' values. The key point is that each instance has its own set of data properties.

Methods (Code Properties)

Unlike data, the methods are stored in the class software, in class-based OOP, or in the prototype, in JavaScript. (As methods require storage space, it would be extremely inefficient to store a separate copy of each method with each instance of the class.)

Methods operate on the data properties of each instance. If each dog had a "message" property, a small breed could say, "Yap, yap" while a large breed said "Woof, woof." If an application's dogs could speak a bit of English, the programmer might combine fixed values with the dog's `name` property to achieve a result like Listing 1-2.

Listing 1-2

```
collie.speak(); // "My name is Lassie."

beagle.speak(); // "My name is Snoopy."
```

Next we put objects to use. Our *JSWindows* system is one example.

Introducing JSWindows

The result you see in Figure 1-1 takes exactly four lines of JavaScript code. One creates the page title and three create the three windows. (Is there a law that says windows must be rectangles?)

The gateway to the online portion of this book is http://www.martinrinehart.com/frontend-engineering/knowits/op/knowits-op.html. You can use the system your self (and enjoy the full color) by clicking "Using *JSWindows*" from the gateway page. Let's take a look.

Windows with Border Radii

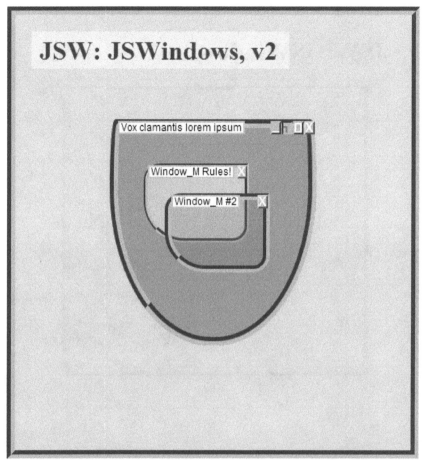

Figure 1-1

The shield in the center of Figure 1-1 is, as you can see from the motto, the frontend engineers' family crest. As you can see from the buttons on its upper right, it is also a window. You can close, maximize, restore and minimize with these buttons (right to left).

The title is also a drag handle.

JSWindows is written in JavaScript for applications on all devices that run HTML4 or 5 and CSS2 or 3. The shapes here are done with CSS3 border radii.

JSWindows Contain JSWindows

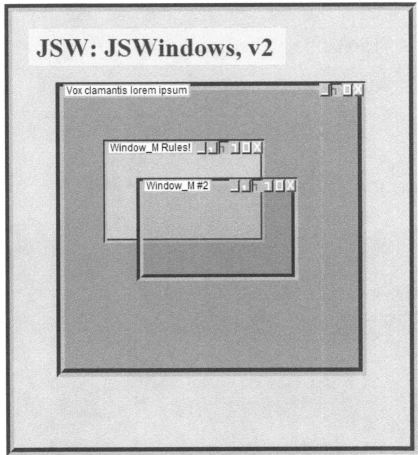

Figure 1-2

In Figure 1-2 we've changed the size of the shield, eliminated the border radii specifications from each window and changed the two inner windows from `Window_M` (window, movable) to `Window_M_BS` (window, movable with buttons for sizing).

Note that there are, by default, three intermediate sizes (between min and max), not just the single "restored" size of some other systems.

We are also using the CSS3 RGBA (transparency) capability for the #2 window.

Click Small, Click Large

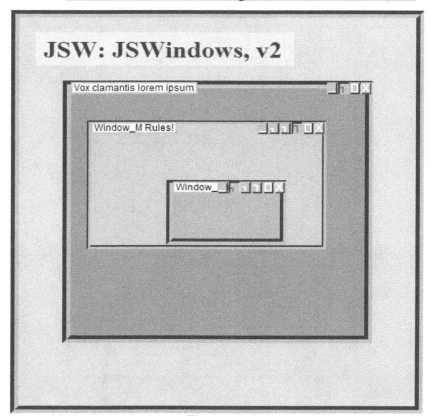

Figure 1-3

Figure 1-3 is exactly two button clicks away from Figure 1-2. Look at the sizing buttons. We clicked the "large" button for one small window, the "small" button for the other.

Next we go on to minimizing. Note that we are minimizing windows within their containers. The shield (the one with the motto) is contained within SCREEN. The two smaller windows are contained within the shield.

Minimized Windows in a Window

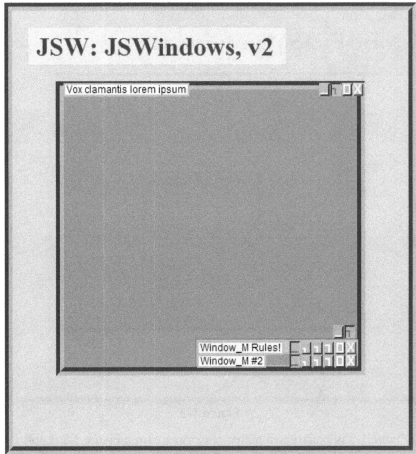

Figure 1-4

Notice that the "minbox" (Figure 1-4, holding the two minimized windows) also has a restore (now disabled) and a minimize sizing button. If you click its minimize button, the minbox is reduced to a one-pixel-tall box, topped by its own sizing buttons, taking almost no screen real estate.

But let's return to the windows with the CSS3 border radii. They're more fun.

The Original Windows, Almost

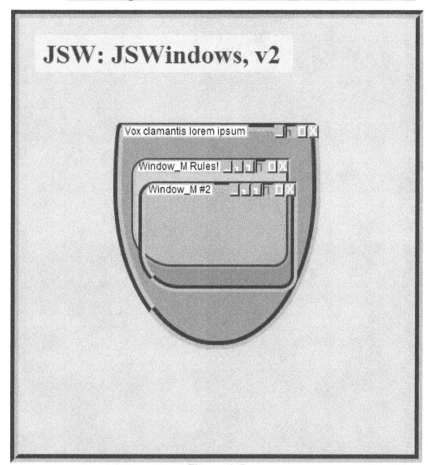

Figure 1-5

In Figure 1-5 the original windows are shown, except that the two smaller ones are still sizable. Here their "large" buttons have been clicked.

Maximizing in the Shield

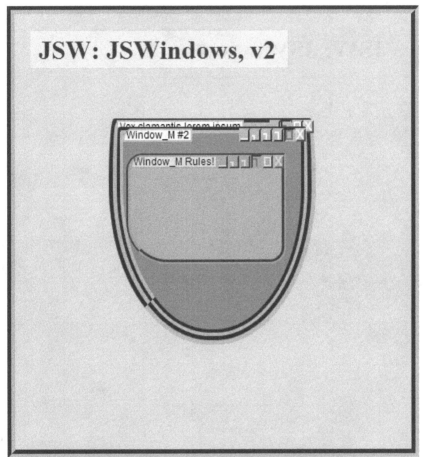

Figure 1-6

In Figure 1-6, we clicked the "maximize" button of the translucent window. (If you compare with Figure 1-5, you can see that the "Window_M Rules!" window is masked.)

Isn't this the way you would have coded "maximize"? (It's easier than you might guess. It works inside circles and ovals, as well as shields, too.)

JSWindows is more fun, and in full color, when you try it online http://www.martinrinehart.com/frontend-engineering/knowits/op/knowits-op.html.

The *JSWindows* system is programmed with class-based inheritance, using long inheritance chains typical of class-based languages. (It does not use OOP-emulating library code, nor the JavaScript prototype chains typical of library OOP implementations in JavaScript.) We return to this system frequently as we discuss the implementation of inheritance in JavaScript.

In Chapter 2 we back up, beginning at the beginning.

2 JavaScript Objects

We begin, in this chapter, by looking at JavaScript objects, how they are created and how their "prototypes" work.

Built-Ins

Programmers new to JavaScript quickly learn that there are common needs that are met by built-in JavaScript "objects." For example, common mathematical operations are performed by the `Math` object's methods.

Math

You want to round a number to the nearest integer. Listing 2-1 shows an example.

19

Listing 2-1

```
var width =
    content_width + padding + border_width;

div.style.width = Math.round(width) + 'px';
```

The `Math` "object" is really just a collection of library functions, all related to mathematical operations. You should not manipulate it as an object.

Date

The `Date` constructor returns real objects, time stamps that include both date and time to the nearest millisecond. The `Date` also provides the methods you want to manipulate dates (to set a time for an appointment next week, for example). The bit of code in Listing 2-2 might be included when you were comparing the running times of alternative methods.

Listing 2-2

```
var start = new Date();
var result = sample_long_function();
elapsed = start - new Date();

alert('Time was: ' + elapsed);
```

The programmer is teased by these built-in objects. Hopefully, you decide that you want to go further and create your own objects.

Ex Nihilo Objects

In JavaScript, you can create objects from a constructor (from the equivalent of class software as in C++) or from a prototype (as in Self). JavaScript combines both. It also lets you create an object *ex nihilo* (from nothing).

There are two direct ways to create a JavaScript object from nothing. You can use the `Object` constructor or an object literal.

The Object Constructor

In JavaScript there is an object constructor, `Object`.

```
my_object = new Object();
```

As the name suggests, this creates an object. The initial capital letter tells you that the `Object()` method was intended for use after the `new` operator as a constructor. When you create an object this way you can assign properties, as Listing 2-3 shows:

Listing 2-3

```
my_object.size = 'large';
my_object.color = 'blue';
```

Veterans of static, class-based languages (such as C++, Java and many others) find this capability novel. They are accustomed to names and types of object properties being fixed at compile time. Dynamic properties (as in Python) remove this restriction. (Static properties give optimal performance. Just-in-time compilation—a technique pioneered in Self—minimizes any speed difference, however.)

The prototype (discussed below) of objects created from nothing is `Object.prototype`.

Object Literals

Listing 2-4 shows another way the above *ex nihilo* object could be created.

Listing 2-4

```
my_object = {
     size: 'large',
     color: 'blue'
};
```

As in C, use of whitespace is for readability. The following line does the same job.

```
my_object={size:'large',color:'blue'};
```

JavaScript object literals also create instances of the `Object` family (as if you used the `Object` constructor) and their prototype is, again, `Object.prototype`.

The object literal notation (documented by Crockford as JSON, JavaScript Object Notation) is still the preferred method for creating objects from nothing. The `Object` constructor has been assigned powerful new capabilities by the most recent versions of the JavaScript standard (ECMAScript). You will want to consider these new capabilities when they become universally available.

Objects created from the `Object` constructor and objects created from object literals all share `Object.prototype` as their prototype. This gives them all, for example, a `toString()` method that reports "[object Object]," telling you that the type is "object", its constructor is `Object`. (This is almost never helpful. Creating custom objects lets you supply useful `toString()` methods. If you `alert()` or `console.log()` an object you will be looking at its `toString()` version. You usually know that it is an object.)

More *ex nihilo* Objects

Functions and arrays are also objects in JavaScript. Whenever you create a function (named or anonymous, with the `function` keyword or the `Function` constructor), you create an object. When you create an array (via the `Array` constructor or the array literal notation) you are also creating objects.

This is another way of creating an *ex nihilo* object:

```
arr = ['dog', 'cat', 'mouse'];
```

From now on, however, we will reserve the adjective *ex nihilo* for objects that are neither functions nor arrays.

Custom Objects

To create your own objects, ones that will have their own prototypes (the next section), you write your own constructor functions, just as you do in class-based languages.

In JavaScript you can begin in much the same way that OOP programmers begin, by writing a constructor function.

Constructors

By convention, the name of a constructor begins with a capital letter. The constructor function assigns properties, commonly data properties, and adds initial values. Listing 2-5 shows a simple example.

Listing 2-5

```
function Dog(name, breed) {
    var new_dog = this; // the 'new' object

    new_dog.name = name;
    new_dog.breed = breed;
}
```

If you chose the parameter names carefully, chances are those same names are also good names for the object's properties. (Study the example to convince yourself that this does not lead to ambiguities.) The pattern in Listing 2-5, where the value of the parameter name becomes the value of the name property, is very common.

Assigning Initial Property Values

Using your Dog constructor, your Dog objects can start their lives with two properties, name and breed, and each Dog will have values for those properties. Listing 2-6 shows this constructor being used to create Dog objects.

Listing 2-6

```
var snoopy = new Dog('Snoopy', 'Beagle');
var lassie = new Dog('Lassie', 'Collie');
```

Familiar object.property notation can be used to access these properties' values.

```
alert(snoopy.breed); // 'Beagle'
```

Non-Trivial Property Values

In addition to assigning arguments passed into the constructor, the constructor can create any properties that you wish. This could include arbitrarily complex computations. In class-based OOP programming, the object's property names and types are specified by the class software at compile time. In JavaScript, the constructor function serves this requirement. (In Self, the properties, "slots," could be added whenever the programmer chose. As in Self, in JavaScript, and other languages such as Python, the properties are dynamic and may be changed, added or deleted, during execution. Only the property values may be changed in traditional class-based OOP languages.)

In JavaScript, the values you assign to properties can include any JavaScript values, including other objects. You could assign functions as property values, but this would seldom be useful. If your constructor assigns functions, it will be assigning the same code to every object it creates. You normally want the function code to be part of the object's prototype (as it is part of the class software, in class-based OOP languages).

Methods as Prototype Values

Methods (functions) can be assigned as object properties, but that would be wasteful. The method code can be assigned to the prototype where it can be accessed by all objects that are members of the family (generated from the same constructor).

A data property could also be assigned to the prototype, but that, too, would be wasteful. Assume you have several types of animals and they have diets such as "carnivore" and "herbivore." Putting this data value into the prototype would make it available to all animals of each type, as Listing 2-7 shows.

Listing 2-7

```
Dog.prototype.diet = 'carnivore';
alert(lassie.diet); // She's a 'carnivore'.
```

The lookup, however, is not needed. In `lassie.diet`, JavaScript looks to the `lassie` object for a property named "diet." It does not find it. Then it looks to the prototype, where it finds the value it seeks. If the property value is the same for all family members, the property can be made a property of the constructor (shown in Listing 2-8), saving the wasted lookup.

Listing 2-8

```
Dog.diet = 'carnivore'; // not Dog.prototype
alert(Dog.diet); // same for Lassie, Snoopy...
```

The JavaScript usage of the constructor is almost identical to the OOP programmer's use of the class software. Instance data is assigned to each object. Methods, and data that applies to the whole family, are part of the class software. (`Dog.diet` is `'carnivore'`; `lassie.diet` is `undefined`.) Instance methods are part of the prototype for the convenience of using `object.method()` calls, for example, `lassie.speak()`.

Now we take a longer look at object prototypes, risking repetition in favor of being absolutely clear.

Object Prototypes

When JavaScript sees an object property name, such as "color" in `object.color` it looks to the object for a property of that name. If the name does not exist it looks to the object's prototype for a property of that name. (The prototype is another object.)

Assume that you created singers, as Listing 2-9 shows.

Listing 2-9

```
function Singer() {}; // no properties
var patty = new Singer(),
    maxene = new Singer(),
    laverne = new Singer();

patty.sing(); // error, undefined method
```

We have no `sing()` method, so these girls don't know how to sing. In Listing 2-10 we teach Patty, individually.

Listing 2-10

```
patty.sing = function () {
    alert('...boogie woogie bugle boy...');
}
patty.sing(); //...boogie woogie bugle boy...
```

Patty can sing, but her sisters cannot. We should have put this
method in the prototype, as in Listing 2-11.

Listing 2-11

```
Singer.prototype.sing = function () {
    alert('...blows eight-to-the-bar...');
};
maxene.sing(); // she sings!
laverne.sing(); // she sings, too!
```

How did we know that `Singer.prototype` was the prototype for
our singing sisters? The prototype for any object you create from a
constructor is the property named "prototype" of the constructor
function from which the object was instantiated. If `Singer` is the
constructor, then `Singer.prototype` is the prototype for `Singer`
family objects. (Chapter 9 fills in all the details of the underlying
mechanism by which `Singer.prototype` becomes the prototype
for all `Singer` family instances.)

In the class-based model, instance methods are written in the class
software. In Java you would have created a `sing()` method in the
`Singer.java` module. In JavaScript you assign the `sing()` method
to the `Singer` function's `prototype` property. The result is the
same. The objects created from the constructor can `sing()`.

(The Andrews Sisters—Patty, Maxene and LaVerne—had their biggest hit, of many,
with "Boogie Woogie Bugle Boy" in 1941. http://www.dump.com/andrewssisters/,
2:21)

The Prototype Chain

Now we repeat the paragraph that started the previous section:

> When JavaScript sees an object property name, such as "color" in
> `object.color` it looks to the object for a property of that name.
> If the name does not exist it looks to the object's prototype for a
> property of that name. (The prototype is another object.)

What happens if JavaScript does not find the name in the prototype? "The prototype is another object." Simply read the paragraph again. JavaScript will look in the prototype's prototype. In JavaScript, all objects you create are either created from the `Object` constructor, and therefore `Object.prototype` is their prototype, or their constructor's prototype is an object created from `Object`, or their constructor's constructor is an object created from `Object`, and so on.

Searching prototypes stops at `Object.prototype`. This is called the prototype chain. Ultimately, `Object.prototype` is the prototype of every object you create, directly or indirectly.

Bear in mind the following two important facts as you consider the prototype chain. First, there are large families of objects (not ones that you create) that may not have prototypes. JavaScript does not know how to do input or output. It depends on a "host environment" for all I/O. Most commonly, JavaScript runs in a browser that provides the host environment through objects. These are called "host objects" and unless the browser's authors were meticulous (most weren't) the host objects do not have prototypes. Host objects seldom have prototype chains.

Second, you can see how the prototype chain could be used to implement inheritance. If you could connect your `Extend` family objects so that properties not found in `Extend.prototype` would be sought in `Base.prototype`, you would have inheritance. What does not follow is that this would be a good way to achieve inheritance. There are other ways that are preferable.

Many authors suggest you use the prototype chain to achieve "prototypal inheritance." In a language such as Self, creating one object from a prototype object is referred to as "inheritance." In JavaScript, creating objects *ex nihilo* involves no inheritance. Creating objects via a call to a constructor is analogous to creating objects in class-based OOP. (JavaScript's *ex nihilo* objects inherit from `Object.prototype`, so they aren't really *ex nihilo*.)

Is the term "inheritance" appropriate for creating objects from a constructor? In OOP, creating base objects from the `Base` constructor is not called inheritance. That term refers specifically to the creation of objects from a family such as `Extend` that "inherits" from a family such as `Base`. In fact, you can code JavaScript as if the prototype were part of an OOP family. *JSWindows* is coded this way. Object methods can be found in their prototypes but properties not in the prototype simply do not exist. (Assume that there is no prototype chain. A property not found in the prototype does not exist.)

The only extensive use of the prototype chain is made by programmers who wish to provide fundamental additions to a JavaScript built-in class. For example, you might wish to add a capability to all `Array` objects. You could add additional method(s) to `Array.prototype`.

Most experienced JavaScript programmers are opposed to this idea. What happens if one library adds extensions to `Array.prototype` and another also adds extensions to `Array.prototype`? We have lots of new capabilities and we're all happy until one library's author inadvertently (and inevitably) picks the same name chosen by another. Then we are in trouble. Whichever code is loaded last gets ownership of that duplicated name. The library that depended on the first-loaded (and therefore overwritten) version of that name becomes buggy. The history of JavaScript is replete with once reliable libraries that suddenly became buggy because of these naming conflicts.

It follows that if the prototype chain is not used for modifications to JavaScript basics and it is not used for inheritance, the prototype chain could be removed from JavaScript. It could and *JSWindows*, for one, would not miss it. (*JSWindows*, as we will see, uses extensive inheritance, none of it using the prototype chain.)

In you want to experiment with Self-like object prototypes, in *JavaScript: The Good Parts* Crockford advocates them and provides a function to create true prototypal inheritance. (It only takes a half dozen lines of JavaScript.)

Now that we have introduced JavaScript objects, we can look at JavaScript's object programming (OP) capability which we will use constantly. Before we go on, let's put this much to use.

Coding a Class

Ready to start writing code? In this chapter and the next four we have guided programming tutorials. The road map is this:

- Create a useful `Box` class (here in chapter 2).
- Add a `styles` configuration object using object programming (3).
- Create a `Borders` class and combine it with `Box` objects using composition (4).
- Create a `Button` class that inherits from `Box` (5).
- Add a `Maskable` capability and an `implements()` method that adds this capability to a `Box` (6).

A) Create Your Template

If you already have a template, or your editor/IDE can create one, test it against these requirements. Upgrade as needed. If need be, create a new template.

A minimal HTML template will include at least:

- A doctype
- File path and name comments
- `<html>`, `<head>` and `<body>` tags
- `<title>` in the head
- `<script>` at the end of the body
- "`use strict`"; in the script

Compare your template to the one at http://www.martinrinehart.com/frontend-engineering/knowits/op/op-tutorial/op-tut-2/op-tut-2a.html. Make sure that yours is better than ours. (But don't overload it with bits you might not need.)

B) Add a Class Skeleton

Turn your template into an HTML file. We'll be working continuously on this one file for all the tutorials in this book. Place it in some convenient folder.

Now we start to write JavaScript.

Every class will need a constructor, an `init()` method (property of
the constructor, not in the prototype) and a `toString()` method (in
the prototype). Add these and compare against our sample at
http://www.martinrinehart.com/frontend-engineering/knowits/op/op-
tutorial/op-tut-2/op-tut-2b.html.

C) Add Parameters

Now we need to think about the actual work for our class. That
means deciding on the parameters for our constructor. Think
carefully here, but don't get stuck. (Think like a backpacker. "When
in doubt, leave it out.")

Our sample includes a

- `parent` (`document.body` or another Box)
- `id` (unique, for the DOM element and for our own use)
- `pos_size` (left,top, width,height array)
- `color` (background)

The `init()` method should copy these parameters into properties of
the `new_box`. Writing these with the `toString()` method will let
you test your work this far. (A simple test is in our sample.)

Our sample is at http://www.martinrinehart.com/frontend-
engineering/knowits/op/op-tutorial/op-tut-2/op-tut-2c.html. You'll be
able to find our samples ("Next" on the right, bottom or the letter on
the menu) without any more links, we hope.

D) Finish `Box.init()`, Add a Mainline

To finish `init()`, `document.createElement()` a `div` as a
`Box.delem` (DOM element) property. Give it an ID (with your `id`
property). Add to the `delem`'s `style` property: a background color
and styles for your position and size values. Don't forget to add a
`position` style (`absolute` or `relative`). And don't forget to
`appendChild()` it to the `parent` element.

Now convert that `alert()` message to an actual mainline, with sensible values in the `pos_size` property. Run. Fix typos. Repeat until you have a `Box` on the screen.

It's good to see your work on the screen. This is always the point where we start to smile. Test out your `pos_size` array with different positions and sizes. Convince yourself that your `color` works. (Create more than one `Box` as you test.)

E) Add Styles

Next chapter we'll do a little object programming, using a `styles` configuration object. For now, we just add styles to the mainline. We use `textAlign`, `fontSize` and `padding`. Go ahead and add any that you like. (We'll do a `Borders` class in Chapter 4, so you might skip border styles for now.)

F) Finish the Mainline

And finally, finish your work with some content in the `Box`. Extra credit if you don't slavishly follow our example.

You've now coded a constructor and an `init()`, so you can inherit from it easily. And you've added an instance method (`toString()`) to the prototype. Not quite ready to graduate from the School of JavaScript OOP, but well on your way.

Now, on to object programming. It's easier to do than to say.

3 Object Programming

We are now ready to consider object programming (OP), the fundamental difference between JavaScript and OOP languages. *JSWindows* makes continuous use of object programming. (An early attempt to write *JSWindows* without OP was abandoned. It may have been possible, but the extra effort was not in our time budget.)

In class-based object-oriented programming the objects are defined before they are created. Once an object exists, you can execute its methods or assign values to its data properties. But you cannot add or delete properties or change methods, for examples. Object programming gives you the ability to do these, and more.

OP Defined

The OOP model combines object instances, sets of name/value pairs, with class software. The class software provides a routine to create

instances, to store instance methods and it provides other services.
This is a subset of object programming, which includes these
abilities.

- An object programming (OP) system allows the creation,
  modification and disposal of objects during program
  execution.

- Objects are collections of properties. Properties are
  name/value pairs.

- "Modification" of objects means the ability to create, modify
  and delete properties. Modifying properties includes
  modifying names and/or values.

- An OP system also provides for services provided by OOP
  classes, such as storing data and code at the class software
  level (to avoid duplicating either in each instance object).

Note that by this definition, the JavaScript OP model is incomplete
as it does not allow direct modification of property names. (It takes a
three-line utility function to modify a property name. A direct
approach to modifying the name would be preferable, but you can
live without it.)

Programming with Properties

JavaScript leads programmers into object programming, almost
without their being aware of it. It's two ways of identifying object
properties play a major role.

Dot Notation

In the familiar `object.property` notation, a period separates the
object reference from the property name. The latter is a constant in
source code.

```
var x = object.prop_name;
```

In the above, "object" is the name of an object reference. "prop_name" is the name of a property of that object (directly, or via its prototype or prototype chain).

This is the common OOP notation, as well. Few OOP languages have the equivalent of JavaScript's subscript notation.

Subscript Notation

Subscript notation allows the use of variable property names. First, with a constant, the above example is repeated here.

```
var x = object['prop_name'];
```

Listing 3-1 shows an example of an expression used to select a property.

Listing 3-1
```
var e = func_returning_string(args);
var x = object[e];
```

Listing 3-2 shows both notations being used to create a new property within an object. Constant and variable property names are shown.

Listing 3-2
```
Object.new_prop = value;
Object['new_prop'] = value;

var e = func_returning_string(args);
object[e] = value;
```

The pair of features above provides surprising power and grace when programming.

Object Programming Examples

Object Sum

JSWindows uses "styles" objects to hold lists of CSS styles. These are the JavaScript versions of CSS declaration lists. Each name/value

pair in the object corresponds to a CSS property name and value.
This is a styles object:

```
{borderWidth: '8px', borderColor: '#a0a0ff'}
```

As styles become known, they are added to an object's styles object.
We often want to add the properties of a new object to an existing
object in the process. Listing 3-3 shows this situation in pseudocode.

Listing 3-3

```
var bstyles = borders.get_styles();
all_styles += bstyles; // pseudocode
```

The += operator does not apply to objects, but we can write a sum
function to do the same job. We want the styles in the incoming
bstyles object to add new properties to the all_styles object. If
properties of the same name already exist in all_styles, we want
to replace their values. As Listing 3-4 shows, this is more trouble to
explain than to code.

Listing 3-4

```
sum = function (old_object, new_object) {
    var ret = {};

    for (var prop in old_object) {
            ret[prop] = old_object[prop]; }
    for (prop in new_object) {
            ret[prop] = new_object[prop]; }

     return ret;
} // end: sum()
```

This function creates a new, empty object. Then the first for/in loop
copies the old object's property names and values into the new
object. The second for/in loop copies the new property names and
values into the new object. In the process it will create new
properties, if required, or override existing properties where there is
a name conflict.

If your project wants a sum() function where the values in the old
object are preserved (not overridden by values in the new object) it is

simple to modify the above. As you loop through the properties of `new_object`, just check:

```
if (old_object[prop] === undefined) ...
```

Do not overwrite the existing property if it is already defined.

OP for Inheriting Prototypes

We also use the `sum()` function to copy prototypes, underneath the `extends()` function. The latter provides a meaningful name and saves typing, two reasons worthy of our support. Listing 3-5 shows `extends()`.

Listing 3-5

```
extends = function (extend, base) {
    extend.prototype = sum(
        extend.prototype,
        base.prototype);
}
```

OP in the *JSWindows* Library

For those who have not totally understood the idea (and for those who are asking, "Is it really that simple?") we provide additional examples of object programming from the *JSWindows* library.

DOM related

The library functions are divided into a "DOM related" group, for dealing with the browser's host environment, and a "Utility" group, for everything else. Almost 80% of both make use of some form of object programming. Listing 3-6 shows the function that deletes a single DOM element. This would be simpler if one browser's bugs did not make it necessary to assign null to the deleted reference.

Listing 3-6

```
delete_delem = function (delem) {

    while (delem.firstChild) {
        delete_delem(delem.firstChild);
    }
    delem.parentNode.removeChild(delem);
    delem = null; // Some MSIE needs this.

} // end: delete_delem()
```

The delete_delem() function calls itself recursively to remove
children from the delem (DOM element). When the children are
gone, it removes the selected element from its parent. As JavaScript's
main use is for DOM manipulation, it shows how OP is an integral
part of its job.

For a second example, Listing 3-7 shows the library function that
attaches an event listener to a DOM element. As with so much
DOM-related work, one of its jobs is to smooth over differences
between browsers. As with so many of these differences, Internet
Explorer, especially older versions, is the problem.

Listing 3-7

```
/** Add an event listener. */
listen_for = function (
        wobj, event_name, func) {
    var delem = wobj.delem;

    if (delem.addEventListener !==undefined) {
        delem.addEventListener(
                event_name, func, false); }
    else if (delem.attachEvent !==undefined) {
        delem.attachEvent(
                'on' + event_name, func); }
                // IE before 9
    else { delem['on' + event_name] = func; }
        // old school!

} // end: listen_for()
```

Again we are working with object properties, in this case, event listening methods. Here we use both dot notation and subscript notation as we fall back to progressively older ways of adding the event listener.

An interesting feature of this library function is that the Wobj reference (Window object, the root of our family hierarchy) is passed as an explicit parameter, Fortran style. We prefer to call these functions in the object style:

```
wobj.listen_for(event_name, func);
```

Listing 3-8 shows the method in Wobj.prototype that lets us use our preferred style.

Listing 3-8

```
Wobj.prototype.listen_for = function (
        event_name, listen_func) {

    listen_for(this, event_name,
            listen_func);
}
```

When you call object.method(), the object reference on the left is converted to the this parameter within the method. We simply put `this` back into the Fortran-style parameter list, explicitly. That gives us object-style method calling for our Fortran-style library functions.

Our third, and final, example from the DOM-related library functions removes an event listener that had been added by the old-fashioned method:

```
element.onclick = click_func;
```

Listing 3-9 shows the listener removing function.

Listing 3-9

```
/** Remove solo listener. */
    stop_listening_on = function (
            wobj, type, func) {
    var delem = wobj.delem;

    delem['on' + type] = undefined;
}
```

JavaScript's subscript notation makes this job simple.

Utility

We have been big fans of object programming for a long time so it came as no surprise that most of our DOM-related utilities manipulated object's properties. After all, the DOM is an object tree. What we were surprised to find was how many of our utility (non-DOM) functions also used OP. We'll start with a simple example.

Whenever we write a constructor, we also write a `toString()` method. It seems you always want to have a readable version of an object as you are developing. But what about your *ex nihilo* objects? The default `toString()` (from `Object.prototype`) reports that you have "[object Object]" (an object created by the `Object` constructor). This is almost never helpful. Listing 3-10 shows a simple utility that creates a readable version of an object that is frequently helpful.

Listing 3-10

```
o2s = function (obj) {
    var ret = [];
    for (var pname in obj) {
        var prop = obj[pname];
        if (typeof prop !== 'function') {
            ret.push(pname + ': ' + prop);
        }
    }
    return 'object{' + ret.join(',') + '}';
}
```

This loops through the properties by their names (in pname) and, if they are not functions, pushes them onto an array of property name/value pairs, as strings. That array is used as the center of the returned string.

Listing 3-11 shows an example of object programming applied to arrays. (Arrays are objects, in JavaScript.) It removes an element from an array, shortening the array by one (ensuring that there are no undefined elements created).

Listing 3-11

```
remove_element = function(arr, element) {

    var index = find_index(arr, element);
    if (index === -1) { return; }

    ret = [];
    for (var i in arr) {
        if (i !== index) { ret.push( arr[i]; )
    return ret;

} // end: remove_element()
```

One of the most common mistakes in any object programming is to assign a second reference to an object when a second object is needed.

```
var not_really_second = first;
```

When `not_really_second` is changed, the same change appears in `first` as they are both references to a single object. Making a shallow copy of `first` is normally correct.

```
var not_really_second = shallow_copy(first);
```

Listing 3-12 shows our `shallow_copy()` function.

Listing 3-12

```
shallow_copy = function (obj) {
    var ret;

    if (obj instanceof Array) { ret = []; }
    else if (obj instanceof Function) {
            ret = obj; }
    else { ret = {}; }

    for (var name in obj) {
            ret[name] = obj[name]; }

    return ret;
} // end: shallow_copy()
```

The code that copies arrays and non-array objects is identical except that the return value is initialized differently. The calling code does not care. Note that using a `for/in` loop to copy the array correctly handles sparse arrays and arrays that have been modified via `splice()` calls.

For those new to shallow and deep copying, a "shallow" copy means that values that are references to other objects are copied. A "deep" copy would duplicate the objects and arrays referenced. During a shallow copy, statements such as the following are executed:

```
copy.prop_name = original.prop_name;
```

This creates a second property with the same name and value as the first, but it is totally separate. After the assignment, there is no connection between the two. It's as if we had `lassie.breed = 'Collie'` and `snoopy.breed = 'Beagle'`.

If the code subsequently assigns to the copy, it does not impact the original.

```
copy.prop_name = some_other_object;
```

The above statement replaces the value of `copy.prop_name` with another object reference. It has no effect on the value of `original.prop_name`.

We are now equipped to consider inheritance in JavaScript, both class-based and prototypal. Before we start on code, we will take a close look at what is really meant by "inheritance" when programming with objects. But first, let's do a little object programming. You will be an ace in a few minutes.

Coding Object Programs

We'll be working with objects. To test our work, we'll want to take a look at our objects. If we use an object where it will be coerced to a string (such as in an `alert()` or `console.log()`) JavaScript may tell us that it's an "[object Object]." (An object made from the `Object` costructor, as every *ex nihilo* object is.) This is seldom helpful. We want to look at the properties of the object. So we begin with a simple, hard-working utility to tell us more.

A) Object to String

We'll use an `o2s()` function (object to string) constantly as we develop. It's job is to take an object, any object, and list its properties. We want the name and value of each property. (You'll want a smarter `o2s()` if you need to show function objects, as their values—the function source code—tend to be very long.)

The `for (name in object)` loop iterates through any object, returning each property's name. Try using it to write an `o2s()` function. Test it with object literals:

```
alert( o2s({breed:'Beagle', name:'Snoopy'}) );
```

Don't fuss overly much with the beauty of the output. It's only for use during development. And it's only for use with objects that don't have a nice `toString()` method, which can do a much better job.

Our version is shown at http://www.martinrinehart.com/frontend-engineering/knowits/op/op-tutorial/op-tut-3/op-tut-3a.html.

B) A `get_ps_styles()` Function

Next, we'll want to put together our `Box`'s styles in the `init()` method, adding `styles` objects as we go along. Right now, however, the body of `Box.init()` is rather crowded with the dull work of turning a `pos_size` array into CSS style specifications. We've moved this into an inner function whose job is to take the `pos_size` array and return the CSS we need. (A value of 100 for `pos_size[0]`—left—becomes "`left: '100px'`".)

Take a peek at ours, if you like, and then write your own. Test it with an `alert()` or `console.log()` inside the `Box.init()` method.

C) A Library Function to `sum()` Obects

Our new `Box.init()` will do its work by the `sum()` library function. You want to write and test your `sum()` carefully, as this one will definitely be at the heart of your production code. Don't forget any of these:

- `sum( {}, {foo:'bar'} )`
- `sum( {foo:'bar'}, {} )`
- `sum( {foo:'bar'}, {foo:23} )`

You can look in the code (3, C) if you haven't a clue where to start. (And you can look back a few pages in this chapter, for a second opinion.) You'll find that `sum()` is hard-working, but that doesn't mean it's hard to code.

Note that the sum operation is not commutative. `sum(a, b)` is not equal to the `sum(b, a)` if a and b have like-named properties. In the third example, above, the value of `foo` will be 23 after the sum, as properties of the second object override like-named properties of the first object. This becomes important in `styles` objects as we want styles we explicitly define to override default styles.

D) Putting `sum()` to Use

Begin by replacing the `color` parameter with a `styles` parameter. (Three places: in the parameter list in the constructor, in the `Box.init()` parameters and in the argument list in the constructor's call to `Box.init()`.) Styles will be a configuration object you can use to specify any CSS styles you like. In your mainline, replace the color specification with an object, like `{backgroundColor: '#c0e0ff'}`. Don't forget to replace the line `new_box.color = …` with `new_box.styles = …`.

Replace the part of `Box.init()` that assigns values to your `delem`'s `styles` object. This takes more thinking than code. Ensure that the specific styles from the `styles` configuration object override any other styles. (Do you want to look at our version first? That's fine. But write your own! This is a very fine example of a little bit of OP making short work of a hard task.)

Our new core of the `Box.init()` method is woefully lacking in comments. That's your job. Feel free to copy our code but add enough comments so that a maintenance programmer will be able to make sense of it.

In the end, test by adding to the styles configuration object. Any style explicitly specified in `styles` should override anything else. For example, you should be able to right align text with appropriate styles.

E) Teach `toString()` About Styles

We've laid the groundwork and made this one easy. The `toString()` method should now be able to show the styles you include in your `styles` object. You've already got the `o2s()` method that will make this easy.

F) A Mainline with Styles

As a next-to-last step, replace those explicit assignments from the work you did in Chapter 2 with assignments to a `styles` configuration object. (This has very little real value with just one box. Picture dozens of boxes, each using one of a handful of different styles objects. That will give this approach lots of value.)

At this point you should have a system that relies on styles configuration objects and you can happily forget the fact that someplace, deep inside, these are assigned to a `delem.style` object.

G) An `alert()` to Test

Finally, if you `alert()` or `console.log()` your boxes, you'll see `toString()`s showing readable styles objects.

Now we can move on to inheritance.

4 Inheritance

Before discussing ways to implement inheritance, and alternatives for achieving its benefits, we have to define inheritance. As class-based inheritance involves classes, we have to carefully define the meanings (on close inspection we find three meanings) of that term.

When we say "object-oriented programming" or "OOP" we are not speaking of general programming using objects. We are speaking specifically of programming in a language such as Java or Visual Basic that uses the C++ style object model, correctly called "class-based" (but commonly called "classical"). This chapter provides definitions leading up to "inheritance" in both OOP and JavaScript. We will see both implemented in JavaScript in Chapter 5.

Classes

There are three definitions of "class" in OOP and JavaScript in this
book:

> A class is a group of objects (we'll call it a "family") that share a
> common set of properties.

> A class is the set of properties shared by such a group.

> A class is the software that creates and supports such a group of
> objects, including the constructor and methods that instances of the
> class can perform or, in JavaScript, the constructor and its
> properties, such as the property named "prototype".

In practical code the first definition usually means the objects created
from a single constructor. You can create such classes in JavaScript
or any OOP-based language. A `Window` in *JSWindows* is an object
created by the `Window` constructor (and therefore, a sibling to other
members of the `Window` class). To avoid ambiguity we will use the
word "family" to describe this type of class.

The second definition will be used when we look at classes (object
families) more theoretically, such as in drawings showing property
groups. We also refer to these as families when the context is not
ambiguous.

The third definition applies to a C++ (or Java, VB and many others)
"class," the software that defines objects. In JavaScript, the
constructor function and its properties serve this purpose. Most class-
based languages also allow class software to have its own data and
method properties. We will call this type of class the "class software"
or an "OOP class" if we wish to speak specifically about OOP
language class software.

In a system written in Java, an object created from the constructor in
`Window.java` would also be called a member of the `Window` class
(we will call it the `Window` family), and that would be very similar to
a JavaScript member of the `Window` family. However, the OOP class
(the class software) cannot generally be manipulated during
execution; it is not an object. The JavaScript constructor and its
properties can be manipulated during execution and is indisputably
an object.

The class-based languages are not all the same, of course. In Chapter 6 we discuss the multiple inheritance of C++ and the somewhat comparable interfaces employed in Java.

Constructors

In class-based OOP there is one method in the class software that is called the "constructor." The constructor's job is to create objects, instances of the class (members of the family). Consider this example using a constructor to create an object instance:

```
fido = new Dog('Fido');
```

The "constructor" is the method named "Dog" that creates a new Dog-family object. Constructors are at the heart of class-based class software, such as Java modules. In JavaScript, any function may be a constructor but the convention is to name constructors with an initial capital letter and to not name any other functions that way.

In class-based languages, constructors create and return class instances (family members), often with the "new" keyword. In JavaScript, "new" is an operator that appears much like the same word in C++ or Java. (Chapter 9 digs deeply into JavaScript's new operator.)

Instance Methods

Instance methods are the verbs of object programming. Listing 4-1 shows examples.

Listing 4-1

```
dog.bark(); // "woof, woof"
sir_paul.sing(); // "Yesterday, all my..."
```

Unlike data properties, for which space is allocated for each object instance, these methods are part of the class software. (It would be extremely wasteful to repeat the same method code with every object instance.) In JavaScript, methods are normally part of the object's prototype (Chapter 3) which is the prototype property of the constructor. The `bark()` method above would be referenced by `Dog.prototype.bark`.

In OOP languages, the instances' methods are normally fixed at compile time. In JavaScript, you could replace these methods during execution, delete them or even change them into data properties. Methods can even be attached to individual objects, so your `Beatle` family could have results like those in Listing 4-2.

Listing 4-2

```
john.sing(); // "Lucy in the sky, with..."
paul.sing(); // "Michelle, ma belle..."
george.sing(); // "While my guitar gently..."
ringo.sing(); // "In an octopus's garden..."
```

(This result can be achieved in OOP languages. It cannot be done, however, by attaching individual methods to objects.)

Class (Family-Wide) Properties

In class-based OOP, class software modules are like objects in that they may have their own data and method properties. These are properties of the family, not of any single instance of the family.

Data

Class software may have its own named data properties. These are called "class static" values in Java. In JavaScript, properties of the constructor serve the same purpose. There is only one data value for each class data property. (There is one instance value for each object instance, whether there are zero or millions of instances.)

Methods

As with data properties, class software may also have its own methods. These operate on the class software's data properties. In JavaScript, function properties attached to the constructor can serve the same purpose.

We can now define inheritance.

Class-Based Inheritance

We will draw class families as ovals, like Venn diagrams referring to sets. We will be referring to object property names. (These do not refer to property values. The "Collie" named "Lassie" and "Snoopy", the "Beagle," are both instances of the Dog family having identical properties such as name and breed. They have different property values.)

Property Sets

The property names of families E and B may be disjoint (no names in common), overlapping (some names in common) or one may be a superset of the other.

Figure 4-1 shows families that share some property names.

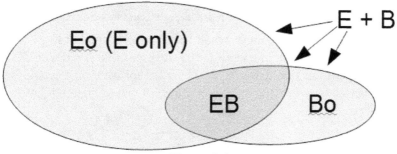

Figure 4-1

In this example, families E and B have some property names in common (area EB) and other properties that are not shared in Eo (E only) and Bo (B only). Next, we turn to the inheritance case, where Bo is an empty set.

Figure 4-2 shows family E (Extend) having a superset of the properties of family B (Base).

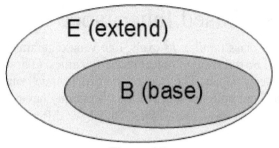

Figure 4-2

In class-based OOP, when Bo is empty we say that E "extends" B, or
E "inherits from" B. class-based OOP designs focus on inheritance,
deliberately seeking this type of family relationship. We will show an
inheritance hierarchy such as the one in Figure 4-2 this way:

In the E class software there would be a statement such as E
extends B, in Java, or class E: B, less readable (even with
access qualifiers omitted) in C++. The class software for E would
then define only the extending properties, shown in Figure 4-3 as E
minus B.

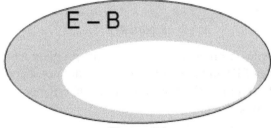

Figure 4-3

The "hole" holds the additional properties, defined in separate class
software that defines B. It is filled in when we specify that E
extends B or B is "inherited" by E.

Constructing an Extending Instance

To create an instance of an extending family, the constructor of the base family, B, is executed first. The constructor of the extending family, E, then runs, adding additional properties. (The additional properties may require computations using the values of the base properties.)

Overriding Properties

We could create properties in family E that had the same names as properties in family B. These properties in the extending family would "override" the same-named properties in the base family. There are times, however, when we will want both. The toString() method is one common case.

A toString() method is usually programmed for every OOP or JavaScript family. This method shows the object's family name and its key property names and values. (toString() methods are invaluable when debugging.) When family E extends B, its base family, we want our toString() to report like this:

```
E{ B{B's properties} E's added properties }
```

That embeds the toString() of B within the toString() of E. We will, on occasions such as this, want to call overridden methods from base families. (Some OOP languages and some copycat JavaScript libraries use "super" to refer to base families. We object. In the first place, the base family is a subset, not a superset, of the extending family. Additionally, using any term, even a well-chosen term such as "subset," to refer to the immediate base family does not give us access to families arbitrarily far back in an inheritance chain.)

Inheritance Chains

An extending family can be used as a base family by another extending family, this way:

Figure 4-4 illustrates this.

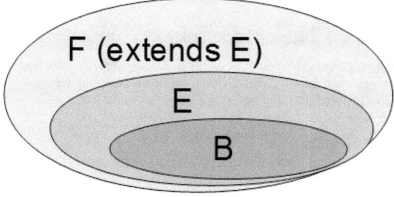

Figure 4-4

The diagram shows that reference to "the subset" of family F is ambiguous. E and B are both subsets of F. Note that this is not multiple inheritance, shown in Figure 4-5 and discussed in Chapter 6. In multiple inheritance, there are two base families, independent of each other.

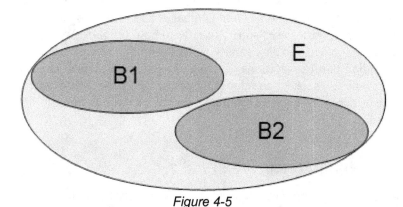

Figure 4-5

In an inheritance chain, there are no independent base families like those you see in Figure 4-5.

In our *JSWindows* system system, the `Wobj` (Window object) is the common ancestor of all families that place objects in the visible window of the browser. The `Rect` family (screen rectangles) inherits from `Wobj`. A basic `Rect` is extended, by the addition of a closing "X" button in the right-top corner, to be a `Window`. This is extended, in turn, by the addition of a title (it serves as a handle for dragging) and move logic to be a movable `Window_M`. The addition of various sizing buttons (min, max and intermediate sizes) gives us a movable, button-sizable window: `Window_M_BS`. To summarize:

```
Window_M_BS
    Window_M
        Window
            Rect
                Wobj
```

Each family except `Wobj` extends a base. Each family except `Windows_M_BS` is the base for an extending family.

This is a typical example of how inheritance is designed into systems, creating progressively more complex objects by extending simpler ones. These designs, and *JSWindows* is no exception, are often force fitted. (Suppose you wanted a window that could be minimized, but was not movable. Sorry.) This chain also hints at how messy the inheritance chain can make methods that attempt to use overridden inherited methods. The `toString()` method for `Window_M_BS` must access each of the extended families' `toString()` methods. You will see that JavaScript makes this quite simple.

Prototypal Inheritance

Prototypal inheritance, pioneered in the Self language, uses the word, "inheritance," but with a different meaning. In Self there are no families. Objects inherit directly from each other. The base object is called the "prototype" of the inheriting object.

A Self object is said to "inherit" from its prototype object. Snoopy might inherit from Lassie. If Lassie had properties (in Self these are called "slots") for `name` and `breed`, Snoopy would start life with slots for `name` and `breed` (and the values would be, respectively, "Lassie" and "Collie"—Snoopy would need fixing).

In OOP, the properties of Lassie and Snoopy would be defined by the `Dog` class software. Neither would start life with property values. Commonly, the constructor would be passed these values when the `Dog` object instances were created. In OOP, these properties are not "inherited." Only properties that were originally part of a base family (perhaps `Pet`) are "inherited" by an extending family.

We will use the OOP terminology when we say "inheritance" or "inherits" without qualification. Properties that are part of a base family may be inherited by an extending family. Properties that are part of the `Dog` family are not called "inherited" by `Dog` family members except when we refer specifically to prototypal inheritance (Snoopy inheriting from Lassie).

Inheritance v. Composition

We do not want to seem to endorse inheritance as an architectural tool. In their classic book, *Design Patterns: Elements of Reusable Object-Oriented Software* (1995, Gamma et al), the Gang of Four advise us to prefer composition over inheritance. We do.

Composition in Theory

If an object includes another type of object as a property, it is using composition. This is called the "has a" relationship. In *JSWindows,* each screen object could "have a" border. The border is wrapped into a `Borders` object.

In contrast, inheritance is used when one object "is a" object of some less complex design. In *JSWindows,* a `Window` "is a" `Rect` with an added closing button.

Composition in *JSWindows*

An onscreen object is not a simple thing. Assuming a rectangular shape, you have to consider position and size, borders and background, styles for fonts and text position and behaviors, just to name a few. In the *JSWindows* examples in Chapter 1, you saw three windows. The title was not a window, but it was a visible object. Listing 4-3 shows the code (a single constructor call) that was required to create the page title.

Listing 4-3

```
var h1 = new Wobj( SCREEN,
        'heading_1', 'h1',
        [10,10, 300,40],
        0,
        {backgroundColor:
            'rgba( 250, 250, 250, 0.5 )',
        fontFamily: 'Times New Roman, serif',
        fontSize: '24pt', margin: '10px',
        paddingLeft: '10px',
        paddingTop: '5px',
        paddingRight: '10px'},
        {innerHTML: 'JSW: JSWindows, v2'} );
```

Note that we have carefully minimized the software. The remaining complexity is there because the reality (putting an object on the screen) cannot be further reduced.

The first three arguments specify the parent container, the title (used as an ID internally) and the type of HTML element (in this case, <h1>). The fourth argument is an array for the "pos_size" (position and size) object, specifying [left,top, width,height]. The fifth element, a zero, specifies the Borders object. We will take a look at Borders, but first note that we already have used composition to bring in the parent, the pos_size and the borders.

Why use an object as a property? You do so when the object is too complex for a simple property. Complexity could come in the number of components, or in the behaviors. We'll think about each with our Borders family.

Complex Properties

A Borders object maintains the full specification of the four borders (left, top, right and bottom) of every object to which the CSS box model applies (virtually every visible object). Three properties can be applied:

- width
- type (solid, dashed, groove, etc.)
- color

Each of these can be a single value applying to all four sides, or four values, one for each side. Additionally, corner radii can be supplied. This can be as simple as a single value establishing the radius for all four corners, or it can be a single value for each corner, or a vertical/horizontal pair for each corner. (If you are counting, that's up to four values for each of width, type and color, plus up to eight values for radii: 20 possible values.

Behaviors

For reasons we never understood (reasons that have triggered no end of expletives) the W3C box model insists that the size of an object is the size of its content area. (The area inside the padding. The padding, in turn, is inside the border.) To do any kind of layout, you normally want to know the size of the object, including borders, padding and content. To make this simple (or at least to make it seem simple, from the outside) we fit out our `Borders` with methods such as the ones shown in Listings 4-4 and 4-5.

Listing 4-4

```
Borders.prototype.get_width_left =
        function() {

    if (this.width instanceof Array) {
            return this.width[0]; }

    return this.width;
}
```

(All objects within the *JSWindows* system are part of the `jsw2` namespace object. These references have not been included in the listings unless they are important to understanding the code.) There are, of course, three other similar methods for the other three sides. These are then combined in methods like the one shown in Listing 4-5.

Listing 4-5

```
Borders.prototype.get_width_horizontal =
      function() {

   if (this.width instanceof Array) {
       return this.width[0] + this.width[2];
   }

   return 2 * this.width;
}
```

There is another similar method for vertical borders.

Key to using borders is to be able to output CSS styles from our specification. Outside, this is easy. You just ask:

```
... = xxx.borders.get_styles();
```

This allows you to forget that the `get_styles()` method weighs in at nearly 70 lines! How could something that is so simple (at least in concept) take so much code?

Listing 4-6 shows a single block extracted from the `borders.get_styles()` method.

Listing 4-6

```
if (borders.color !== undefined) {
    if (borders.color instanceof Array) {
        styles['borderLeftColor'] =
                borders.color[0];
        styles['borderTopColor'] =
                borders.color[1];
        styles['borderRightColor'] =
                borders.color[2];
        styles['borderBottomColor'] =
                borders.color[3];
    } else { styles['borderColor'] =
            borders.color; }
} else { styles['borderColor'] =
        DEFAULTS.Borders.color; }
```

If the border colors are specified with an array, we use one value at a time for borderLeftColor, borderTopColor and so on. Or we use a single value for the borderColor. Or, if nothing is specified, we use the DEFAULTS value. Unfortunately, code can be very simple without being short.

This gives you a glimpse of the code behind the Borders family objects. We hope it has been enough to show why an object was required; a simple property or two would not be adequate.

Regardless, we always prefer composition over inheritance, but the latter is our focus. In Chapter 5 we look at the code for implementing inheritance in JavaScript.

Coding Composition

The *JSWindows* Borders class provides such a good example that we decided to do it again for our tutorial example, only to simplify. Our big brother Borders is aware that you can specify all four borders in one go, or provide separate specifications for each border (hence the choice of the plural, "borders," as the class name). To keep our focus on OOP coding, not CSS issues, we're not going to allow separate specifications for each border in this tutorial code. You can expand it on your own.

A) Create a Borders Class

We begin by adding a `Borders` class: a constructor, an `init()` class method and a `toString()` instance method. We build our starter classes in three steps. First, create the skeleton with "params" where the parameters will go. (If you like precision, the "params" are really arguments when the constructor uses them to call the `init()` method.) Second, we expand "params" into an actual list. (This is where you do some thinking. What parameters do you want?) And third, fill in the details. The `init()` saves the parameters as properties of the new object. The `toString()` reports on the more important ones. (Don't be afraid to leave minor items out of your `toString()` methods.)

Examples for this section start online at http://www.martinrinehart.com/frontend-engineering/knowits/op/op-tutorial/op-tut-4/op-tut-4.html

B) Get Styles from Borders

There are any number of reasons to prefer numbers to CSS styles. For instance, if your border width is 5, the overall vertical or horizontal border width is 10. If you want a total height of 100, your content height is 100 minus 10. Simple arithmetic? Very. Possible if your width is "5px"? Not until you extract the number from the string.

We enjoy the simplicity of numbers by only converting to CSS styles on demand. We create an instance method that we can call with `borders.get_styles()` that will return, as a styles-like object, the three borders styles properties. You should be able to do this yourself without looking at our code.

We've used our `get_styles()` method as the heart of a revised `toString()`.

C) Add Borders Defaults

To keep our borders simple, we can have all our boxes start with default borders. That will eliminate the need for a borders parameter to the `Box` constructor (or a borders value in a configuration object). To generalize (or at least to hint in that direction) we start with a `DEFAULTS` object and let the `Box init()` get values from the `DEFAULTS`.

D) Create a `Box.set_styles()` Method

If you look ahead you'll realize that a `set_borders()` method will be needed if you ever want to use a non-default border. That will be easy enough, but how will the new border specifications find their way into the DOM styles? One well-organized way will be to move the styles logic out of `Box.init()` and into its own `set_styles()` method that could be called by `Box.init()` and after setting new border styles.

This has the added advantage of moving an algorithm that could get tricky into its own function where it will be easy to work on if problems arise. (*JSWindows*, for example, assumes that your specified sizes for a visible rectangle are the sizes including borders and padding, not just the content sizes. So when borders are changed, styles for width and height also change.)

E) Create a `Box.set_borders()` Method

With the `Box.set_styles()` method ready, it's easy to add a method to set new borders. It just takes the new border color, style and width and uses them to create a new `Borders` object. Then it calls `Box.set_styles()` to do all the work.

Ready for class-based OOP inheritance? In plain JavaScript? That's next. Hope you won't be disappointed when you find out how simple it is.

5 JavaScript Inheritance

When family E extends B, an instance of E has some of its own data and method properties, and it acquires the data and method properties of family B. Instance data properties are commonly assigned by the constructor and instance methods are commonly made available in the prototype. In this chapter we show how JavaScript—plain JavaScript, library functions not required—can successfully use its hybrid class/prototypal object model to create class-based OOP inheritance hierarchies. These do not require, and do not really want, JavaScript's prototype chain.

We are not endorsing inheritance-based architecture; we just want to demonstrate, for the benefit of veterans of class-based OOP languages, that it is simple to create inheritance hierarchies in JavaScript.

Cascading `init()` Methods for Data

If you cannot use the base family's constructor, how can you achieve inheritance of data properties? There is a simple solution: moving the logic out of the constructor into methods that you write. For our initialization code, we write methods we name Xxx.`init()` (where Xxx is the name of the constructor). They do whatever we tell them to do, leaving JavaScript constructors to handle the assignment of prototypes and nothing more. If you were creating a Dog with a constructor such as the one in Listing 5-1:

Listing 5-1

```
function Dog(name, breed) {
    var new_dog = this;

    new_dog.name = name;
    new_dog.breed = breed;
}
```

We would change that to the two functions in Listing 5-2:

Listing 5-2

```
function Dog(name, breed) {
    var new_dog = this;
    Dog.init(new_dog, name, breed);
}
Dog.init = fuinction(new_dog, name, breed) {
    new_dog.name = name;
    new_dog.breed = breed;
}
```

You'll see how this enables inheritance in a moment. More generally, if the parameters needed by family B are b1, b2 and so on, the `init()` looks like Listing 5-3.

Listing 5-3

```
function B(b1, b2, ...) {
    var new_b = this;

    B.init(new_b, b1, b2, ...);
}

B.init = function(new_b, b1, b2, ...) {
    new_b.b1 = b1;
    new_b.b2 = b2;
    ...
}
```

Function B is a constructor, to be used after the new operator. This function (by rather complex "magic" explained in Chapter 9) makes B.prototype the prototype object for each instance it creates. B.init() is a reference to a non-constructor function. (As a property of B, it is like an OOP class (family-wide) method. Instance methods would be properties of B.prototype.)

When the calling code creates an instance of the B family, nothing is changed.

```
var b = new B(b1, b2, ...);
```

However the logic is all external to the constructor, available to an extending family's constructor. The highlighted line in Listing 5-4 shows the call to B.init() from an extending E.init().

Listing 5-4

```
function E(b1, b2, e1, e2, ...) {
    var new_e = this;
    E.init(new_e, b1, b2, e1, e2 ...)
}

E.init = function(new_e, b1, b2, e1, e2, ...) {
    B.init(new_e, b1, b2);
    new_e.e1 = e1;
    new_e.e2 = e2;
    ....
}
```

Here the E (extending) family's constructor logic (in E.init())
starts by calling its base family's constructor logic (in B.init()).

Note that B.init() and E.init() are not constructors. They are
properties of constructor functions. In OOP, these would be family-
wide methods. Note also that a family that extends E will not even
need to know that E extends B. Simply calling E.init() will be
enough. Whether E stands on its own or extends a long chain of other
families will not matter.

A Theoretical Example

The gateway to the online portion of this book is
http://www.martinrinehart.com/frontend-
engineering/knowits/op/knowits-op.html. The "Master Classers" link
takes you to inheritance code from Crockford, Edwards, Flanagan
and Ressig. That code is compared to using plain JavaScript. We
show the plain JavaScript solution here. A family hierarchy is
proposed: C extends B and B extends A.

```
C
      B
            A
```

The ability to run overridden methods of extended families is tested
by requiring the toString() of family C to access the

`toString()` of family B which, in turn, accesses the `toString()` of family A.

The A constructor assigns, through `A.init()`, two parameters to properties of the base family, as Listing 5-5 shows.

Listing 5-5

```
function A(p1, p2) {
    A.init(this, p1, p2);
}

A.init = function (inst, p1, p2) {
    inst.a = p1;
    inst.b = p2;
}

A.prototype.toString = function () {
    return 'A{' +
        'a=' + this.a +
        ',b=' + this.b +
    '}';
}
```

Note that the value of the parameter `inst` (as in "object instance") in the `init()` method is the value of the `this` pseudo-parameter of the constructor.

We move on to show how family B extends A. The B constructor has four parameters, the first two for the base family, A, and the next two for the extending family, B. It also has a method, `toString()`, that overrides the method of the same name in the base family. This was deliberately complicated by the requirement that the `toString()` of the extending family had to access the `toString()` method that it overrode. Listing 5-6 shows that this does not require a lot of code.

Listing 5-6

```
function B(p1, p2, p3, p4) {
    B.init(this, p1, p2, p3, p4);
}
B.init = function (inst, p1, p2, p3, p4) {
    A.init(inst, p1, p2);
    inst.c = p3;
    inst.d = p4;
}
B.prototype.toString = function () {
    return 'B{' +
        A.prototype.toString.call(this) +
        ',c=' + this.c +
        ',d=' + this.d +
    '}';
}
```

The `B.init()` method passes the first two calling parameters to
`A.init()`. Code that uses an instance of B can use `b.p1` or `b.p3` to
address the data properties, without caring that `p1` is a base family
property and `p3` is an extending family property. The `toString()`
method of an instance of B can be called for a readable report, as
Listing 5-7 shows.

Listing 5-7

```
var b = new B(1,2,3,4);
b.toString(); // "B{A{a=1,b=2},c=3,d=4}"
```

We were never happy that the `toString()` of the extending family
relied on the `call()` function method, but we used it regardless.

The `call()` and `apply()` Methods

There are two seldom used and little known JavaScript methods that
can be used on functions: `call()` and `apply()`. They both do the
same thing. They let the programmer take over from JavaScript and
assign directly to the `this` parameter used inside a function. We
avoid these methods if at all possible because we doubt the
maintenance programmer who "inherits" our code after we have
moved on will be familiar with them. However, they are needed, on
occasion.

To use a function that has no explicit parameters with a custom value for this, use call().

```
any_func.call(value_for_this);
```

The function will be called and this, inside the function, will be assigned the value you specified. (Using call() can be a life saver. JavaScript does not always supply the value you need for this.)

If the function you want to call has one or two explicit parameters (for example, p1, p2) you precede them with your this value:

```
any_func.call(value_for_this, p1, p2);
```

The call() method (it is a method in Function.prototype, so you can use it on any function) will pass along any return value, so you can write:

```
var ret = any_func.call(value_for_this);
```

We use call() (for lack of a good alternative) to get direct access to overridden toString() methods, for example. In Listing 5-8, E extends B:

Listing 5-8

```
E.prototype.toString = function () {
    return 'E{' +
        b.prototype.toString.call(this) +
        // E's other properties here
    '}';
}
```

The apply() function works the same way, except that it provides for a list of parameters of unspecified length. Look it up if you need it; avoid it if you can.

Extending an Extending Family

The last requirement of our theoretical example was to show that a third family could extend the extending family, without knowing or caring that its base family was extending another base. Listing 5-9 shows that it meets this requirement.

Listing 5-9

```
function C(p1, p2, p3, p4, p5, p6) {
    C.init(this, p1, p2, p3, p4, p5, p6);
}
C.init = function (inst, p1, p2,
          p3, p4, p5, p6) {
    B.init(inst, p1, p2, p3, p4);
    inst.e = p5;
    inst.f = p6;
}
C.prototype.toString = function () {
    return 'C{' +
        B.prototype.toString.call(this) +
        ',e=' + this.e +
        ',f=' + this.f +
    '}';
}
```

Here you see the first four (of six) data values passed to B.init() where two will be passed along to A.init(), two will be assigned as B's extending properties. The final two will be assigned as C's extending properties. C will neither know nor care how its base family assigns the first four values.

Similarly, C will use B's toString() to report on the four values that it let B handle. The report will be exactly the one you want, as Listing 5-10 shows.

Listing 5-10

```
var c = new C(1,2,3,4,5,6);
alert(c);
// "C{B{A{p1=1,p2=2},p3=3,p4=4},p5=5,p6=6}"
```

Since using this technique as a baseline to compare against the inheritance library alternatives of Edwards, Flanagan and Resig, we have used it regularly. The *JSWindows* system is one example. We deliberately pushed the JavaScript philosophy (keep inheritance chains short) aside in favor of a long, OOP-style inheritance hierarchy, but the technique showed no problems.

A Practical Example

In the *JSWindows* system, the Wobj (Window OBJect) is the base of the hierarchy of onscreen families.

```
Window_M_BS
    Window_M
        Window
            Rect
                Wobj
```

(The above cascade is a simplification. Button also extends Rect, for example. Button_close extends Button and so on.)

Listing 5-11 is the code in the Window_M_BS constructor. The one line needed to inherit from Window_M is highlighted.

Listing 5-11

```
Window_M_BS = function (...params...) {
    Window_M_BS.init(this, ...params...);
}

Window_M_BS.init = function (new_window,
            ...params...) {

    Window_M.init(new_window, ...params...);

    // sizing button logic here
}
```

Similarly, Window_M.init() will call Window.init(). Window.init() will call Rect.init(). Rect.init() will call Wobj.init(). Every constructor moves its logic into an init() method, and each init() starts by calling the init() for the family it extends.

That technique shows all the code, save for the details. The devil, as they say in politics, is in the details. With *JSWindows*, the devil was in the default values.

Discrete Defaults

We use a SKIN object that the designer can use to tailor colors, sizes and other cosmetics to his or her own designs. Much of the hierarchy can be styled separately. For example, the basic window object, the Wobj, gets a two-pixel, solid border. Window objects get a wider, ridge border. At each step we check to see if a style has been explicitly specified. If not, we use the default styles.

Listing 5-12 shows an example from the Window family.

Listing 5-12

```
if (borders === undefined) {
    borders = new Borders(
        DEFAULTS.Window.border_width,
        DEFAULTS.Window.border_style,
        // etc.
```

The code goes on to add border colors and radii. As a convenience we allow the border width to be specified, and let the other values default, so the default borders block is followed by a similar one that checks to see if borders is a number and then assigns the other defaults. This is not rocket science, but it does amount to quite a bit of code.

Implementing Capabilities

The init() methods in *JSWindows* follow this pattern:

1. Set defaults.
2. Call the base family's init().
3. Add logic.

The logic added includes assigning parameters to properties (object.property = parameter;). If the names are well-chosen the parameter name and the property name may be the same. Then any new capabilities are added. This can be very simple. A Window is a Rect that is Closable (has a closing "X" button, right-top corner). This is the entire logic needed to implement that capability.

```
new_window.implement('Closable');
```

(Of course the `Closable` capability had to be programmed. Figuring out how to place an "X" in a small `Rect`—matching font points to button pixels—took some work. Otherwise it was simple.)

Some times, a small bit of code is required. For example, our window sizing buttons include `min` and `max` with three sizes in between. The in-between sizes are named, not creatively, 0, 1 and 2. By default, if the `button_choices` argument is not supplied, we provide all five buttons, as Listing 5-13 shows.

Listing 5-13

```
if (button_choices === undefined) {
    button_choices =
        ['min', '0', '1', '2', 'max']; }

    new_window.implement(
        'Button_sizable', button_choices);
```

Next we leave the constructors and `init()` methods that provide data property inheritance to look at method property inheritance.

Prototypes for Methods

To have the benefits of class-based inheritance we need to do the equivalent of placing the instance method code in the class software. In JavaScript, with its hybrid class/prototypal model, that means putting the methods into the prototype. (We will also consider alternatives after we see what is required to use the prototype.)

Theory

In Self, objects "inherit" from a prototype object. The arguments in favor of this approach very much resemble the arguments in favor of agile programming. In class-based OOP, considerable effort is required to design the family hierarchies before coding begins. Experienced designers report the same thing: the design is never right. This is no reflection on the skill of the designers. Unanticipated relationships appear between families. Inheritance doesn't work because the subset/superset relationship doesn't hold. Multiple base families appear where the design tried to avoid multiple inheritance. The code often requires revision deep into its earliest families

(families on which the rest of the system has grown to depend). Refactoring is never as easy as one hopes.

By contrast, the prototypal advocates assert, the way to get started is to create an object that meets your immediate needs, use it as a prototype and build something. You want to get to the point where you start discovering those troubling relationships between your families without having a lot of code already depending on the original design.

In our experience, very few systems contradict the theory that "the design is never right." You learn more by building a system. What you learn usually becomes what you wish you had known when you started. Carefully designed hierarchies generally need refactoring. Does it follow that the prototypal approach is best? Not necessarily. Sometimes a quick prototype is a very helpful learning tool that gets you pointed in the right direction. (It's good to find the right direction when there's still so little code that starting over is no problem.) Sometimes a quick prototype leads you into a trap, but you won't see it until you've "completed" half or more of the system. (Remember what Brooks said. "Plan to throw one away. You will, anyhow." Frederick P. Brooks, Jr., *The Mythical Man-Month*, 1972.)

JavaScript lets you design hierarchies or just make a quick prototype. It is completely agnostic on the subject. The ability to use object programming (Chapter 3) and to substitute capabilities for family hierarchies (Chapter 6) will certainly help, whichever approach you take.

Prototypal Inheritance

Pure prototypal inheritance is easy to code in JavaScript, although the code is cryptic. The idea, if family E extends family B, is shown in listing 5-14.

Listing 5-14

```
E.init = function(new_e, params) {…}

E.prototype = new B(args);

E.prototype.another_func = function ...
```

You assign an object of family B to E.prototype. Then you add the E-specific functions to E.prototype. You have used an instance of B as the prototype for instances of E.

Now, JavaScript will look to E.prototype for properties of an E instance that it doesn't find in the object. And it will look to the prototype of E.prototype (its value is B.prototype) for properties not found in E.prototype. This "inherits" the unknown properties from B. At best, this is sub-optimal.

The properties of B commonly include data and methods. We seldom want data properties that are the same for every object instance. (If you use Lassie as a prototype, you probably don't want Snoopy's breed to be "collie," even temporarily.) We will probably assign values to our new E object that we pass in as arguments to the constructor. If these replace all the B data properties then the B data properties will be merely wasting space in E.prototype. This is inelegant but likely immaterial. The problem is the properties that are not overridden.

Assume you want all instances of E to share data values. A better approach is to assign these shared values to the E constructor.

```
E.shared_property = shared_value;
```

The code will then refer to E.shared_property, making it clear that this is a value shared by all instances, not an instance property. (And it will also eliminate the "didn't find it, look it up in the prototype" step an instance variable would require.)

The conclusion is that assigning a B instance to E.prototype is not the best way to inherit data properties from B. What about methods?

Assume that B's methods were stored in B.prototype. Assigning an instance of B to E.prototype gives instances of E access to these methods, in two lookup steps. An instance of `E` needs to execute, for example, `b_method()`. The code specifies `e_inst.b_method()`. JavaScript does not find a `b_method` property of `e_inst`, so it looks in `E.prototype`. Again, it doesn't find `b_method`, so it looks in the prototype of `E.prototype` (`B.prototype`) where it will find the method it needs.

These lookups are fast, but they should still be avoided if they aren't helpful. Can we do better?

Prototype Inheritance Alternatives

Performance is optimized if we assign references to the inherited methods (in `B.prototype`) to names in `E.prototype`, as Listing 5-15 shows.

Listing 5-15

```
E.prototype.b_meth0 = B.prototype.b_meth0;
E.prototype.b_meth1 = B.prototype.b_meth1;
. . .
```

This approach is requires a bit more programming effort and may be a maintenance issue. (Will this list of inherited method properties be updated when you add a new method to `B`?) A small object programming function, (see Chapter 3), could automate the necessary updates.

Another approach, and the easiest way to get all methods in `B.prototype` into `E.prototype`, is to simply assign a reference.

```
E.prototype = B.prototype;
```

That is easy, but it has one major problem. If you override any method in `E.prototype`, the method will also change in `B.prototype`. As you will almost certainly want `E.prototype.toString()` to be more extensive than `B.prototype.toString()`, you need something better.

JSWindows uses a library function, `extends()`, to add `B.prototype` to `E.prototype`.

```
extends(E, B);
```

The `extends()` utility function is a typing-saving way of calling another utility, `sum()`. The `sum()` function is a good example of object programming. It adds the methods in `B.prototype` to `E.prototype`. Since the methods we say are "in `B.prototype`" are, in fact, references to methods, not the methods themselves, this is exactly what we want. If we want to make a unique version of an inherited method, a new reference will replace the one we need to upgrade.

```
E.prototype.toString = function ...
```

This will not affect the method of the same name in *B.prototype*. (The function on the right, above, is somewhere in memory. A reference to that function is assigned to the left of the equal sign, to the `toString` property of the `prototype` property of the object E. That has no impact on anything in the object B.)

Listing 5-16 shows the technique used in *JSWindows*, combining `init()` methods for data inheritance and object summing for method inheritance.

Listing 5-16

```
Function E(params) {
    var new_e = this;
    E.init(new_e, params);
}
E.init = function(new_e, params) {...}

extends(E, B);

E.prototype.another_func = function ...
```

Note that this is the same logic as in Listing 5-14, except that the highlighted line now sums the prototypes, rather than assigning an instance of the base family. Our execution speed is improved, and perhaps more important, our code readability is dramatically improved. *JSWindows* uses class-based inheritance; it does not use the prototype chain.

Prototype Alternatives

We are still using the prototype, and a single prototype lookup, to access instance methods. We would save CPU cycles by eliminating this lookup (although we doubt it would be enough cycles to have any impact on the user's perception of application performance). Do we have choices?

Library Functions

Going all the way back to Fortran, in the 1950s, we could use the granddaddy of all patterns: the function library. The object method calling syntax is this:

```
object.method(args);
```

The equivalent library function call is this:

```
method(object, args);
```

For any one method, there's very little difference. If you simply prefer the object syntax, well, we do too. And the object syntax lets us reuse one method name for each object family (subtype polymorphism through dynamic binding, if you like details— `duck.talk()` may be a different method than `cow.talk()`, if you like animals).

Prototype Lookups and Performance

Let's consider performance for a moment.

In a visual application (on a monitor, tablet, phone or whatever) "instant" response means "in time for the next screen refresh." Monitors generally refresh 60 times per second. Smaller devices are often faster. At 1GHz (a speed that became the low-end standard in smart phones in 2011) your viewer's CPU clock ticks about 17 million times between screen refreshes. A prototype lookup may waste a hundred or even a thousand of those clock ticks. Can we afford to waste a lookup? The answer is obviously "yes" if we are talking about a single lookup. The answer becomes less obvious when we are talking about multiple lookups in an inheritance chain, and multiple inheritance chains (possibly several for every object on the screen) in a single draw operation.

Consider the three windows we showed in our preview of the *JSWindows* system. Three objects on the screen? Well, there are three windows. But each has a title (another object on the screen). Each has three to five sizing buttons (each another object on the screen). Each window has a closing button. Those sample windows are five to seven objects, each, and they are demo windows, without content. Think about creating medium-sized dialog boxes. You quickly find quite a large number of objects on the screen.

Class (Family-Wide) Methods

Another alternative is to use family-wide methods, not instance methods. This is, in fact, just another way of organizing library functions. Whether you place these functions in a Fortran-style library, or append them in groups to pseudo objects like JavaScript's `Math` object, or address them as OOP class methods (constructor properties, in JavaScript) makes no difference, except to the maintainability of the code.

In general, functions that are specific to a single family are often best organized as family-wide functions, gathered in a single place in the source and accessed with a single prefix (like `Math.round`, `Math.ceil` and so on).

Using family-wide methods is the best approach, but only when the method applies to the whole family. Methods that individual instances perform are best placed in the prototype.

JSWindows Inheritance

JavaScript in general, and *JSWindows* is no exception, still makes extensive use of Fortran-style libraries. (jQuery is the most popular JavaScript library, and with good reason.) Support functions, such as the `extends()` function used for prototype adding in *JSWindows*, are still well-organized this way.

JSWindows also makes occasional use of family-wide methods and regular use of the prototype as a place to store instance methods.

But we do not recommend *JSWindows* as a model for your work. It was deliberately created with an excess of inheritance as a demonstration system. Let's write a little inheritance code first, and then in the next chapter we will look at alternatives to inheritance.

Coding OOP Inheritance

Let's create a `Button` class that inherits from `Box`. This will give us a `Button` built on a DOM `div` element, which has advantages and disadvantages. On the plus side, the DOM `button` element has cross-browser issues. On the minus side, enhancing a `div` will have accessibility issues. (Give your `Button`s a title and half your accessibility issues are resolved. The other half, a focus ability, is not as easy.)

We'll begin by adding a third function to our library. Follow online at http://www.martinrinehart.com/frontend-engineering/knowits/op/op-tutorial/op-tut-5/op-tut-5.html

A) Add a Shallow Copy Utility

You will want to make shallow copies of prototype objects. (Remember, if you simply copy object references you have two references to one object. Changes made by either reference change the single object that underlies both references.) Fortunately, a shallow copy utility is only about a minute of typing if you are marooned on a desert island far from the nearest JavaScript library. Type up one on your own before you look at our sample. (How did we ever get along without object programming?)

Simple tests using `alert()`s should work. (Don't forget empty objects, when you test.)

B) Create a `Button` Class

An extending class is a class. One way to create one is to start as if it were any other class. Write a constructor (one working line), an `init()` method and a `toString()`, all with "params" before you even begin thinking. Then do some thinking and convert the "params" to what you really need.

If you start your `Button` class with the same "params" you used for your `Box` class you will be matching our example.

This class is not ready to test.

C) Inherit `Box` Data Properties

To have all the `Box` data properties assigned to your `Button` (you'll need all of the constructor parameters), just call `Box.init()` from inside `Button.init()`.

We also add a default button background color to `DEFAULTS` (you'll need it for proper mouseover/mouseout behavior) and put it into our `styles` value (if it doesn't already have a `backgroundColor` property).

This class will still not run. It has not inherited `Box` methods yet.

D) Inherit `Box` Methods

We didn't write any `Box` methods to begin. As we went along, we added methods like `Box.get_styles()`. If experience is a guide, you'll be adding more if you put your `Boxes` into use. Making a shallow copy of your `Box`'s prototype is all you need to inherit the `Box` methods (including ones you will write in the future). If you `sum()` `Button.prototype` with `Box.prototype` you get a shallow copy and also preserve the `Button.prototype.constructor` property.

Warning! If your objects are in alphabetical order your `Box` methods are all written before you get to your `Button` class. A shallow copy wouldn't work if your `Button` class came first. The class you copy from must appear in your source before you make a copy, otherwise its prototype will be nearly empty.

 Alphabetical order makes it easy to find things in your code (which gets important when your files get longer) but it doesn't always work. Solving these order problems can be as simple as choosing names creatively, and as ugly as not being able to find what you want. If you need to put your classes out of order, leave comments in the code in places a reasonable person might look. You, yourself, might be the first "reasonable person" to thank yourself for doing this.

With your methods inherited, there is one more detail and you are ready to test. The detail is correctly appending to the DOM. We've appended to `document.body`, so far. For buttons, you want to append to the `delem` of another `Box`. A check for the `appendChild()` method will succeed if the parent is a DOM element, but fail if the parent is a `Box`.

Now you are ready to add a `Button` or two to the mainline. Use your existing `Boxes` as their parents. Remember that the position coordinates are relative to the parent `Box`.

E) Register Boxes

Bear with us for a moment. This is easy to do, but requires some explanation.

There is an issue when you are wrapping DOM elements into your own classes. The DOM elements are "host objects" and you do not want to edit them. The next edition of any popular browser could add exactly the same property that you add, with disastrous results.

The only safe properties of host objects are the ones that are provided intentionally for your use. Fortunately, there is a good supply: `id`, `title`, `alt` and all the event-handling properties, to name a few. We're fond of using `id` as it lets us maintain a registry of our own objects, tied to the DOM host objects.

We maintain a registry object. (*JSWindows* calls it the `wobj_list`.) It's property names are the DOM object ids. Its property values are our own wrapper objects. If you have a box, id "box1", to register:

```
var box_ref = new Box(parent, 'box1', ...);
    ns.registry['box1'] = box_ref;
```

When an event (a mouse click, for example) happens on the DOM element (`box_ref.delem`), the `this` in the event handler is a reference to the DOM element and its id is, in this example, 'box1'. Listing 5-17 shows us getting the element reference:

Listing 5-17

```
function click_handler(event) {
    var delem = this,
        my_box = ns.registry[delem.id];
...
}
```

With this explanation, add a line to your code just after you create the namespace object that creates a property named "registry". Then add a line that assigns a reference to the "new_box" in Box.init() to your registry, like:

```
    ns.registry[id] = new_box;
```

Yes, that's object programming at its best. Simple. Powerful. Try not to gloat when your Java-writing friends ask you what it does.

An alert() showing an o2s() of your registry will show a growing registry (though it will be tedious if you have many boxes in your mainline).

F) Customize Properties

Those ugly default Box borders are now ugly Button borders, too. So you want the Button.init(), after it calls Box.init(), to overwrite the borders property, picking values you added to a button property of the DEFAULTS object. You decide if all (or almost all) your buttons will have one style (use it for your DEFAULTS) or if you will want custom styles for most buttons (make your DEFAULTS stand out, not necessarily in a good way).

Those Buttons you added to your mainline should look better now.

G) Add Custom Methods

Normally, you would want to customize the base class's methods. In this case, the base class's methods (Box.set_borders(), for example) are just fine. But we do need to add custom event handlers for the DOM objects. Our buttons need to look and feel like buttons when a mouse pointer wanders over them (and wanders back away from them) and they should perform their assigned duties when they are clicked. For starters, simply saying, "You clicked me." is a good idea during development.

For this code, using "on" handlers (`onclick()`, for one) will be acceptable. See *JSWindows* for using more modern handlers.

Your `Buttons` should suddenly look and feel like buttons.

With these handlers, you have created a simple, OOP-inheritance style extending class, `Button`, and used your `Box` class as a base class. If you look back over the code, you'll probably be surprised at how very little effort it took. Use one of your `Button`'s `set_borders()` methods (a method inherited from `Box`, even if you didn't remember it) to convince yourself.

6 Inheritance Alternatives

C++ permits "multiple inheritance." We cover this next. Java simplified C++ and multiple inheritance was one of the advanced features it left out. In its place, Java featured "interfaces," originally documented as a sort of poor man's substitute for multiple inheritance, but in the end they proved far more valuable. (In Chapter 8 we show that interfaces are now commonly cited as one of the main OOP concepts. Multiple inheritance is not.) We extend interfaces to "capabilities" which borrow from and extend both Java's interfaces and JavaScript's "mixins." Capabilities also allow a convenient replacement for multiple inheritance.

Multiple Inheritance

Many times you meet objects that combine the features of simpler objects. C++ (among others) allows an extending family to have multiple base families. This is both powerful and problematic. There were good reasons for Java to exclude this feature. Figure 6-1 shows the basic idea.

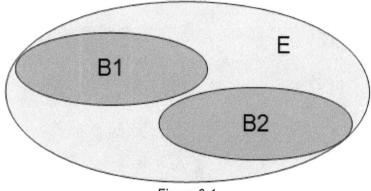

Figure 6-1

The intent is obvious. You want a third family, E, to include the properties of two base families. In Figure 6-1 those families are B1 and B2.

With two base families, you must decide which constructor runs first: B1 or B2. In C++ the compiler runs whichever you named first as an extended family in, for example:

```
class E: public B1, public B2 {...}
```

Of course, real base families are probably not named with convenient integers that tell you which should come first. And real base families have inconvenient issues, such as the constructors of both having circular dependencies. (A property in B1 depends on values in B2 and vice-versa.) Or suppose both base families have the same name for different methods. If those problems seem simple, consider the diamond-shaped inheritance hierarchy where B1 and B2 both extend a single family while another extends B1 and B2.

The diamond pattern is common when modeling reality. Consider B1 and B2 in Figure 6-2.

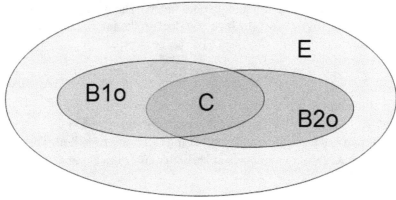

Figure 6-2

Forget E for the moment. If inheritance is a major design tool, when two classes overlap there is an easy reaction: give the overlapping properties a class of their own, and have the others inherit from a common base (B1 and B2 both inherit from C, in Figure 6-2).

```
E
        B1, B2
            C
```

When you then consider E, you have a diamond inheritance issue. (Many C++ programmers avoid multiple inheritance entirely.)

Java simplified the class-based model by replacing multiple inheritance with interfaces.

Interfaces

An interface is the API, the outward facing properties of class software, with methods defined as "signatures" but not implemented. The class-based signature includes the method's name, return type and the types and order of the parameters. (JavaScript methods have nothing comparable for types, both an advantage and disadvantage of having dynamic typing.)

A classic Java interface is Runnable, the interface required for an object to create a new thread. It contains exactly one method: run().

The method has no return and no parameters. The thread is created with a `Runnable` object. In Java you declare the interfaces that a class implements with the `implements` keyword:

```
class foo implements Runnable; // Java code
```

The thread knows that a `Runnable` object can be told `object.run()`. When an object is passed to the `Thread` constructor, the compiler checks that it has a `run()` method. That means that `object.run()` is at least guaranteed to begin execution of a method.

JavaScript has no way of enforcing such a guarantee. In practice, we have a Java-emulating thread package that has the same requirement for a `run()` method. Our thread-based test loads correctly but fails immediately if the `run()` method is missing. In theory a failure before execution begins would be even better, but in practice there is very little difference.

In Java, interfaces commonly end with the "able" suffix. A `Runnable` object is an object that is able to "run" (by calling its `run()` method). A list of objects of the same type can be sorted if the family implements `Comparable` (by providing the comparison method the sort routine requires). `Comparable` objects are able to be compared. The simplest Java interface is `Serializable`. It is an empty interface (nothing is required) that tells Java it is OK to write the object to disk for persistent storage. (This is a promise from the class software's author about the ability of the class software, made to the authors of other class software.)

Capabilities

In Java, when you declare that class software implements an interface, you need to write method bodies for the methods that the interface requires. In JavaScript, we write "capabilities" which combine the defined interface (the programmer must enforce its requirements) with the data and method bodies that support the interface. Capabilities also use a little object programming to attach required methods and properties to the host object.

We use the term "capabilities" as an implemented interface provides a capability. In Java, when you implement the `Runnable` interface you create an object that is capable of being run. When you implement the `Comparable` interface your objects are capable of being compared (for sorting, for example). Our capabilities are an object-programming enhanced way of implementing interfaces in JavaScript.

Unlike Java, our JavaScript capabilities can add properties to the objects that implement them. To avoid confusion, we permit a capability to add exactly one property, with the same name as the capability, to the object implementing the capability.

In *JSWindows*, a `Window` is a `Rect` that implements `Closable`. (To the user, it presents an "X" in the right-top corner. Clicking the "X" closes the window.) In the code the `Closable` capability outfits the `Rect` with the "X" and the attendant logic. (It closes the window when clicked. It also highlights itself—giving a red glow—when the mouse hovers over the "X".) To make a `Rect` `Closable` the code is simply:

```
new_window.implements('Closable');
```

Our *JSWindows* was originally intended to use pure class-based inheritance. We gave up. The main object hierarchy uses class-based inheritance, but almost all the objects are outfitted with capabilities, code written using significant object programming. This lets us share capabilities among all the types of windows, for example, saving lots of programming.

If you are using JavaScript "mixins" you have seen the benefits. Our capabilities are mixins that also directly modify the objects with which they are mixed (although in a limited, controlled way).

The Window[_M[_BS]] Problem

To use class-based inheritance we radically simplified our Window-based family hierarchy. Clearly, windows could have more features than simply being movable or button-sizable. We eliminated "closable" by making that a defining feature of windows. We finessed the title by making it the move handle. If you want a title, your window must be movable. Let's quickly design that restriction out.

If we have just three features beyond closable—T (titled), M (movable) and BS (button-sizable)—we have these possible combinations:

```
Window, Window_T, Window_M, Window_BS
Window_T_M, Window_T_BS, Window_T_M_BS
Window_M_BS
```

That is eight possibilities (assuming that, for example, `Window_T_M` is the same as `Window_M_T`). What happens if you add one more capability? (As soon as this book is done we want our window borders draggable, to reshape the windows. Corners too.)

More generally, if you divide your object properties into groups corresponding to the way they may be used by base families, three families could have the four combining property groups shown in Figure 6-3

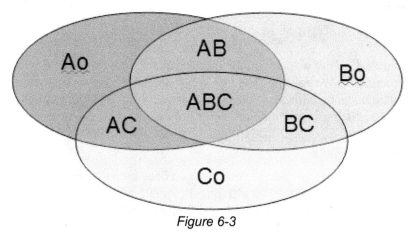

Figure 6-3

("Ao" is a shorthand name meaning "A only.")

There are seven property groups here. Again, suppose you wanted a fourth basic class. Figure 6-4 shows some of the possibilities. (All the possibilities would require drawing in 3D, a feat that goes beyond the printed page or the flat screen. If you like, mentally add regions for AD, BC and so on.)

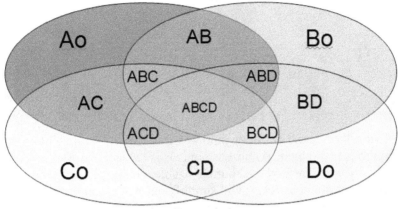

Figure 6-4

We show thirteen separate regions (sets of properties). If you wanted to provide a family hierarchy that allowed any of these combinations you would have one for each region (13), one for each combination of two regions (78 more), and so on. Clearly, an inheritance hierarchy will not solve this problem. Capabilities will.

Returning to our windows, you could have a title capability (T), a movable capability (M) and so on. In answer to our rhetorical question (what happens if you add a fourth capability?) we have a base Window to which we may add any of four capabilities. Assuming we design our capabilities carefully so that they do not conflict with each other, we have added a capability to be used as needed.

The most commonly used combinations can be named, as before. The infrequently used combinations can be created as needed.

Our inheritance hierarchy adds the `Button_sizable` capability to `Movable` windows: `Window_M_BS`. There is no law that says sizing buttons should not be available for non-movable windows, however. Listing 6-1 creates this window.

Listing 6-1

```
custom_win = new Window( ... );
custom_win.implements('Button_sizable');
```

If we wanted a movable, button-sizable window, but had no inheritance hierarchy beyond the Rect, we could create one as Listing 6-2 shows.

Listing 6-2

```
win_m_bs = new Rect( … );
win_m_bs.implements('Closable');
win_m_bs.implements('Movable');
win_m_bs.implements('Button_sizable');
```

Obviously, creating custom windows with exactly the capabilities we require is no problem. Almost as obvious is the fact that if we regularly want the movable, button-sizable window, creating the `Window_M_BS` constructor will simplify our work (and make it easy to add another capability in the future).

Mixins

There is ample precedent for our capabilities in the JavaScript programming pattern known as "mixins." A mixin is a set of properties that you can add to other families, as needed. Assume you want to add titles to some windows (and not to others). A title mixin might have a `set_title()` method for the actual title text and an `add_title()` method which dropped the text into a title box with a nice border, positioned as you prefer.

You would then write code very like our capabilities code, as Listing 6-7 shows.

Listing 6-7

```
my_window.mixin(title_mixin);
my_window.set_title('Title for My Window');
```

You now have a title capability for a window that wants a title, without burdening the rest of your windows with unnecessary methods. And by adding these properties to the window, you avoid adding prototype lookups.

Calling Capability Methods

We want to be able to call our capability methods easily. Two obvious choices are to attach a property with the same name as the capability and call methods of that property, or to call methods of the underlying object. Consider the ability to draw a mask over an object (for use underneath a modal dialog, such as an `alert()`.) We named the capability "Maskable." There are two choices shown in Listing 6-8.

Listing 6-8

```
window.mask(); // direct attach
window.unmask();

window.Maskable.mask(); // property attach
window.Maskable.unmask();
```

Capabilities as Constructor Properties

After some debate we decided against `window.mask`. It certainly looks good, but what happens as you write more capabilities? The probability of name collisions rises from highly unlikely, with a few capabilities, to nearly certain as you create a lot of capabilities. We decided that it was more robust to attach a single property to the constructor (in this case, `Maskable`) and let the capability "own" that property.

Capabilities as Single Properties

The decision to have just one property for each capability has proven itself in practice. The capability can add all the data properties and methods it wants to its own property. There is no more fear about name collisions. (Your application is about the Halloween ball? Go ahead and let your people `mask()` and `unmask()`. It will not conflict with your `Movable`'s masks.)

That decision immediately brought up another question, however. What should be the name of this property? Specifically, we thought both "maskable" and "Maskable" were strong candidates.

We eventually decided to keep the capital letter. JavaScript otherwise has no convention for initial capitals in property names, so the initial capital here (window.Maskable) clearly identifies a family capability.

We feared that this might be confused with the initial capital for a constructor function, but that did not become a problem in practice.

As an aside, JavaScript has very few conventions. We favor adopting more. For example, JavaScript's object property names use "lowerAndUpper" capitalization: `Date.getFullYear()`. To keep our custom properties separate, we use "lower_with_underscore" names: `Pos_size.get_padding_vertical()`.

Capability Prototype Methods

One more capability choice was whether to use family-wide methods (`Maskable.mask()`) or prototype methods (`Maskable.prototype.mask()`). The former saves a prototype lookup. The latter wastes CPU cycles but lets us use our favored `object.method()` syntax.

Again, we chose the latter. Programmers are entitled to think about themselves occasionally. The name "prototype" disappears when you call a prototype method: `wind.Maskable.mask()`. The object becomes an explicit parameter when you call a family-wide method: `Maskable.mask(wind)`.

Examples

We define a `Window` as a `Rect` with a closing button. More precisely, a `Window` is a `Rect` that implements the `Closable` capability. This is the line in `Window.init()` that does the job:

```
new_window.implement('Closable');
```

Simple enough?

We expect that you might ask if we have moved the real work into the `implement()` method. Listing 6-5 shows the entire method.

Listing 6-5

```
Wobj.prototype.implement =
        function (capability_name, args) {
    var wobj = this;

    wobj[capability_name] =
        new jsw2[capability_name](wobj, args);
}
```

Our namespace object, jsw2, has constructors for each capability:
Closable, Maskable and so on. So jsw2[capability_name] is
a way of selecting the right constructor. It is called with wobj, a
reference to the window object that called its implement method,
and whatever args the capability requires. (Closable doesn't
require any.) This simple method handles every capability. Now let's
take a detailed look at the Closable capability.

Closable

We'll start with the code. Listing 6-6 shows the Closable
constructor.

Listing 6-6

```
Closable = function (window, args) {
    var new_closable = this;

    new_closable.button = new Button_close(
            window,
            window.name + '_closable_button',
            [DEFAULTS.Closable.button_left,
            DEFAULTS.Closable.button_top,
            DEFAULTS.Closable.button_width,
            DEFAULTS.Closable.button_height]
    );
} // end: Closable()
```

That's one hundred percent of the Closable code. It creates a new
Button_close, correctly positioned per the DEFAULTS specified.

To be fair, the Button_close does some of the work. It knows, for
example, what colors it should use normally and when the mouse
hovers. It also knows how to respond to a mouse click.

The closing function was interesting. The question was, close the window (discarding it) or simply hide it (`display: 'none'`)? We settled for looking for an `on_close()` function option on the window itself. The button looks for this function and executes it, if it exists. Then it discards the window, unless the `on_close()` returns `false`. In that case, the window is saying, "OK, I've got it." and the closing button's job is done. That lets the window hide itself, if that's what it prefers.

Maskable

We simplified a bit when we said that a `Window` is a `Rect` that implements `Closable`. The Window also implements `Maskable` as our modal dialogs are only modal with respect to the launching window. (That let's the user look at the dialog, move the dialog out of the way to look at other windows/do other actions, and then decide how to respond. "Save? Well, let me check on these other things. I'll let you know.")

Figure 6-5 shows an alert popped up from the shield-shaped window. The default popup was neatly centered over the shield. We used the fact that it was movable before we took this screenshot. Any other windows on the screen would still be available for use. Only the shield is blocked.

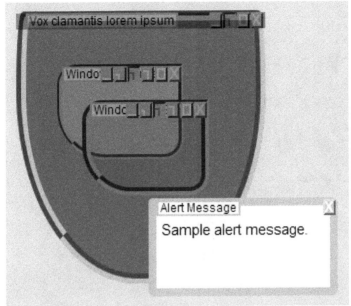

Figure 6-5

A window launches a modal dialog by first launching a mask (translucent, it darkens the window) and then launching the dialog. The mask also grabs all mouse events and discards them, effectively turning the window "off" while the dialog is open.

The code in the window's `init()` is like the `Closable` code:

```
new_window.implement('Maskable');
```

We looked at the `Wobj`'s `implement()` method in the section above. Listing 6-7 shows the `Maskable` constructor.

Listing 6-7

```
Maskable = function (wind) {
     var new_maskable = this;

     new_maskable.wind = wind;
} // end: Maskable()
```

That merely stores a reference to the window in the `maskable` property. This is used by the `Maskable`'s `prototype` methods, `mask()` and `unmask()`. Listing 6-8 shows the `mask()` method.

Listing 6-8

```
Maskable.prototype.mask = function () {
    var maskable = this,
        wind = maskable.wind;

    maskable.modal_mask =
            new Rect( wind,
            wind.name + 'modal_mask',
            [0,0, '1 C','1 C'], 0,
            {backgroundColor:
            DEFAULTS.Maskable.mask_color} );
    maskable.modal_mask.fit_inside(wind);
    maskable.modal_mask.draw();

    maskable.modal_mask_top =
            new Rect( wind,
            wind.name + 'modal_mask_top',
            ['0',DEFAULTS.Window.title_top,
            '1',DEFAULTS.Button.height],
            0,
            {backgroundColor:
            DEFAULTS.Maskable.mask_color} );

} // end: Maskable.mask()
```

This creates two masks. The first is the main mask. It covers the content area of the window, very nicely. The `fit_inside()` method is the same as used by the `maximize()` method. It picks border radii that will correctly fit the inside of the curves of the containing window. The second is an extra mask for the top line of the window. The draggable title and the clickable window sizing and closing buttons may still be available (by default, they are drawn two pixels below the top of the border). We need to make them inaccessible until the modal dialog is closed.

The `unmask()` method, shown in Listing 6-9, performs the opposite function.

Listing 6-9

```
Maskable.prototype.unmask = function () {
    var maskable = this,
        wind = maskable.wind;

    maskable.modal_mask.del();
    maskable.modal_mask_top.del();
    // wind.draw();

} // end: Maskable.unmask()
```

This capability also has a `toString()` method. Carefully fitting the main mask inside the curves of interestingly shaped windows took a bit of work.

Button_sizable

There are, by default, five sizing buttons: `min`, `0`, `1`, `2`, and `max` that you see left of the closing button in Figure 6-6.

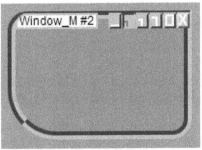

Figure 6-6

(The capability accepts a list, if you don't want all five. For example, `['min', '1', 'max']` would give you a standard min, restore, max set. Our shield used this set, as Figure 6-7 shows.

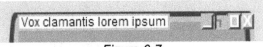

Figure 6-7

In code, three-button sizing could be done this way:

```
new_window.implement( 'Button_sizable',
         ['min', '1', 'max'] );
```

The internals of the `Button_sizable` capability may not concern you. Given the simple call, above, you get the buttons you want, correctly placed (assuming right-top placement suits your needs). Alternatively, you may rewrite some or all of the 300 lines of code that this capability requires. Here we'll discuss some highlights.

The Button_sizable Constructor

The constructor has a main body and inner functions in a support role. We'll discuss the inner functions first.

The `choose_default_button()` function is used when you have specified more than one of '0', '1' and '2' size buttons. If you choose all three, '1' (medium) is the default. If you choose two, and '0' (small) is one of the choices, '0' is the default. The default is assigned the size you initially specify for the window.

Two other inner functions, `size_larger()` and `size_smaller()` are used for the non-default sizes, if any. The larger choice increases both dimensions 1.4 times, which will approximately double the area of the window. The smaller choice shrinks both dimensions to 0.7 times the original size, approximately reducing the area by one half.

Now, back to the main part of the constructor. After some details, it begins by creating a "panel" (borderless rectangle) which will hold the buttons. Then it loops through your button choices, adding the buttons you've chosen onto the panel. It does some non-trivial fussing with positions and sizes to make sure that they align neatly. It also gives them appropriate names that will be used later when they are clicked. (Remember, it is the DOM element that is clicked. We have to find our way from this element to our button object.)

The last function of the constructor is to add properties to the button objects that specify the window's position and size after the button is clicked. These will be available to the button's click handler functions.

The Click Functions

There are three click functions. One for the minimize button, one for the maximize button and one for the other three buttons (viewed from here on as ways of choosing the specific size assigned in the constructor).

The `click_max_func()` comes first (alphabetical order). It creates a set of vars that it will use:

- `delem` is the DOM element (that reports the click)
- `button` is the button object that wraps the DOM element
- `panel` is the panel that holds the buttons
- `window` is our window object
- `container` is the window into which you will maximize

There is a major bit of architecture nearly hidden here. We deal with our own screen objects. Each of our objects (a `Wobj` or a family extending `Wobj`, and they all extend `Wobj`) contains a `delem`, the DOM element. A click, for example, reports the DOM element that was clicked. How do we find our `Wobj`?

The design constraint is that modifying host objects (objects provided by the host environment, and that definitely means DOM elements) is a bad practice. You shouldn't just stick your own properties on to host objects. (Next revision of the browser and you could be unhappily surprised to find that the browser now uses that property for its own purposes.) There is, however, one exception: properties that the host environment expects you to modify. (You may attach a string to the `title` property, for example. That's what it's there for.)

Our design is simple. Each of our objects is created with a `name`. We use this `name` in two places. In the DOM element, it is the ID of the element, a property the host provides us for our own use. When the element is clicked, the element is `this` in its click handler. So `this.id` is the value of the `name` property we have given our own object. The second place we use these names is in the `wobj_list`, a system-wide list of our window objects. The properties in this list use these `names` as their property names, and the property value is a reference to our window objects. So `wobj_list[delem.id]` is our object. JavaScript's objects can provide simple solutions to some complex problems.

Choosable Buttons

The click functions all `choose()` the last button clicked. This is based on the `Choices` utility family. This family groups a list of like objects, one of which is chosen. This is common for radio-type buttons, for the selected window within an enclosing window and for a menu choice, to suggest some examples. When you `choose()` one of the list, another must be shown in its non-chosen state. This is written in classic Java interface style. The objects in the list must all be `Choosable`. A `Choosable` object is one that implements the `choose()` method. To `choose()`, or `choose(true)` requires the object to show itself in a selected state. To `choose(false)` requires the object to show itself in a non-chosen state. Our buttons reverse their borders, from outset to inset and change paint colors from white (enabled) to gray when you `choose()` them.

The Choices object's prototype methods are written in a JavaScript style, as an *ex nihilo* object. Listing 6-10 shows a sample.

Listing 6-10

```
Choices.prototype = {
    /** */
    add: function (item_to_add) {
        var choices = this;

        choices.array.push(item_to_add);
    },
    /** */
    add_and_choose: function (item_to_add) {
        var choices = this;

        choices.add(item_to_add);
        choices.choose_last();
    },
    /** */
    choose: function (choice) {
        var choices = this;

        choices.index = choices.find(choice);
        choice.choose();
    },
```

This prototype object goes on for ninety lines. Most of the functions are as simple as the ones shown here. We like the style as it is very readable, even for JavaScript newcomers who may be new to JavaScript's flexible coding options.

The `Choosable` interface is not expressed in code, unlike a Java interface. It is up to the programmer to add objects that implement `Choosable` (have a `choose()` method) to a list of choices. We wouldn't object to additional compiler support.

The `Button_sizable.Button` Family

```
Button_sizable.Button
    Button
        Rect
            Wobj
```

The `Button_sizable` capability contains two families of its own. The `Button_sizable.Button` extends `Button` (`Button` extends `Rect`, `Rect` extends `Wobj`). Again, our architecture uses excessive inheritance as this is a demonstration project, proving that class-based inheritance style design can be implemented in JavaScript. We would normally use shallower object hierarchies. For example, the `Button` could just extend `Wobj` directly.

These buttons can be `punch()`ed or `unpunch()`ed. Listing 6-11 shows that this is a simple process.

Listing 6-11

```
Button_sizable.Button.prototype.punch =
        function () {
    var button = this;

    button.borders.style = 'inset';
    button.draw();
    button.label_func('gray');
    button.disable();

}
```

The button's `label_func()` draws the lines that show the graphics on the buttons. The `disable()` method turns off the click listener.

With `punch()` and `unpunch()` methods, the `Choosable` interface is very easy to implement, as Listing 6-12 shows.

Listing 6-12

```
Button_sizable.Button.prototype.choose = function
(chosen) {
      var button = this;

    // punch if 'chosen' is true or undefined
    if (chosen === false){ button.unpunch(); }
    else { button.punch(); }
}
```

Programmers not familiar with JavaScript will find this conditional strange:

```
if (chosen === false) ...
```

Commonly, you would test (!chosen). That would be true, unfortunately, if chosen were undefined. Hence the comment in the code.

The Button_sizable.panel Family

The panel that holds these buttons is a member of a separate family. Its code is responsible for positioning its buttons aligned nicely with the closing button. The buttons are loaded into a Choices object named buttons. This makes tasks such as setting the buttons' states very simple, as shown in Listing 6-13.

Listing 6-13

```
Button_sizable.Panel.prototype.choose = function
(button) {
    var panel = this; // the size buttons panel

    panel.buttons.unchoose();
    panel.buttons.choose(button);

}
```

The Click and Draw Functions

The Button_sizable capability includes click and draw functions, also written as *ex nihilo* objects. Listing 6-14 shows the click functions.

Listing 6-14

```
Button_sizable.click_funcs = {
    min: Button_sizable.click_min_func,
    0:   Button_sizable.click_resize_func,
    1:   Button_sizable.click_resize_func,
    2:   Button_sizable.click_resize_func,
    max: Button_sizable.click_max_func
}
```

Listing 6-15 shows two of the five draw functions. The others are similar, except for the drawing details. These objects keep the buttons very well organized, which will be appreciated by the person who needs to add additional button choices.

Listing 6-15

```
Button_sizable.draw_funcs = {
    min: function (color) {
            var button = this;
            if (color === undefined) {
                    color = 'white'; }
            remove_kids(button.delem);
            draw_rect( button.delem,
                    0,10, 9,2, color );
        },
    0: function (color) {
            var button = this;
            if (color === undefined) {
                    color = 'white'; }
            remove_kids(button.delem);
            draw_rect( button.delem, 0,6,
                    4,2, color );
            draw_rect( button.delem, 2,8,
                    2,4, color );
        },
    ...
```

Capabilities Summary

A capability is something which object instances can do. Unlike
methods of a family, multiple families may have instances that are
able to do the capability. The capability is attached to instances as
they are created.

Capabilities may be the distinguishing feature separating an
extending family from a base family. In *JSWindows* the `Window` is a
`Rect` that implements the `Closable` and `Maskable` capabilities.
Because they are independent of any family, however, capabilities
may still serve other families. (A `Text` family, wrapping the HTML
`<textarea>` element, might also implement `Maskable` if it had a
need for modal dialogs.)

By creating a distinct functional unit, capabilities help achieve the essential goal of all object programming: to separate parts of longer program units into the shortest possible programs.

Coding a Capability

Capabilities may be the next step past Java's interfaces in important object programming developments. It's too early to tell. Certainly they build on JavaScript's mixin pattern which has proven itself repeatedly as an excellent use of object programming.

For this tutorial, we pause for a look at the design before we start programming.

Design the Capability

Capabilities are a new thing. We want to repeat the design you've seen in this chapter. We'll use the `Maskable` capability (the ability to draw a temporary mask over an underlying application component while a modal dialog is waiting for input).

To check if a `Box` is `Maskable`, you should be able to ask:

```
if (box.Maskable !== undefined) { ...
```

To make a `Box` `Maskable` you simply:

```
box.implements(Maskable);
```

To draw a mask over a `Maskable Box`:

```
box.Maskable.mask();
```

And to remove the mask:

```
box.Maskable.unmask();
```

(Namespace object omitted for clarity.)

To generalize the above, replace "Maskable" with "Capable" where "Capable" is the name of any capability. Capabilities will be attached directly to the object namespace: `ns.Capable`, for instance.

A) Code the `implements()` Method

We've found it convenient to make the `Maskable` method a
constructor (capital "M"). The `implements()` method is a `Box`-
class instance method, allowing you to say:

```
box.implements(Maskable);
```

To enable this, build your name into the `Maskable` class:

```
Maskable.capability_name = "Maskable";
```

(That statement looks circular. Look more carefully and you see that
it is not. The name of the object reference, "Maskable" in this case, is
not part of the object unless you put it there.)

Our method is very simple, and a powerful argument for the merits
of object programming. It is online at
http://www.martinrinehart.com/frontend-engineering/knowits/op/op-
tutorial/op-tut-6/op-tut-6a.html.

B) Program the Capability

The capability code is relatively simple. Your `implements()`
method passes a reference to the `Box` that gets the capability. Your
capability attaches a property of its own name to the `Box`. The
`Maskable` capability attaches a `Maskable` property, for example.
Then you attach whatever data and methods you like to that property.

The only wrinkle in this is that when your calling code specifies, for
example:

```
box.Maskable.mask();
```

The `this` in the `mask()` method is a reference to the object you
know as `box.Maskable`. To find the owning `Box` object you must
create a reference to it. (When you write `foo = new Bar();` your
`new` object has no hint about your reference's name, unless you
somehow pass the name to it. For example:

```
foo = new Bar("foo");
```

We call the reference to the `Box` the owner of the `Maskable` property. Then the `box.Maskable.owner` is the `Box`, itself.

Once you complete this step, you have completed the programming tutorials, although you have not completed the `Maskable` capability. You have, however, completed all of that capability except the code inside the mask() and unmask() methods, which have nothing left that concerns capabilities. This is plain (not simple, but plain) JavaScript DOM manipulation code. *JSWindows* has the code you need if you want to go forward with this on your own. We recommend, however, just using *JSWindows*.

To test yourself, try another capability. Pick one you will need for your own work. Use this `Maskable` capability as a template.

Adding a Mask

The joy of writing a capability is that once it is completed, it is trivial to attach it to any suitable object. The object must possess whatever properties the capability manipulates, obviously. But if the object has those properties, your job is done.

The sorrow of writing a capability is that you must still roll up your sleeves and write some code. In concept, adding a mask is simple. You launch a new DOM element, using `rgba()` translucency, above the element you wish to mask. The mask element traps and discards all events. (Modal dialogs are launched above the mask.) In practice this is only simple if all your content areas are strictly rectangular and you don't mind unmasked borders sticking out around the mask. (These look awful. Try it if you must see for yourself.)

In Figure 6-5 you saw a two-part mask covering a shield-shaped window and its top-line title and buttons. We refer you to the *JSWindows* source code (online at http://www.martinrinehart.com/frontend-engineering/knowits/op/jswindows/source/op-source.html) for all the details. The inside of a radiused corner, by the way, is itself a radiused corner where the radius is exactly that of the outer enclosing corner minus the width of the border. (That part only looks hard. Using multiple border widths with radiused corners is currently beyond the capabilities of most modern browsers.)

Removing a Mask

This is as simple as removing an element from the DOM. You just delete the mask element and you are done. Right? Unfortunately, that is not as simple as it should be because of bugs in older versions of one major browser.

If you delete an object that has children, you make all that object's children orphans, subject to garbage collection. They will go away, almost magically, in due course. In the bad old days, you had to delete them yourself.

Welcome back to the bad old days. To delete an object from the DOM without leaking memory in buggy browsers, you must recursively delete all the object's children. To delete them from the memory-leaking browser, set your JavaScript references to null. *JSWindows* library function `delete_delem()` does this job. You are still left with uncollected JavaScript references to null, but that is trivial compared to uncollected DOM element references.

Next, we conclude with some summary thoughts on how you should use and avoid inheritance in your JavaScript systems.

7 Designing for JavaScript

We chose the *JSWindows* project because it was well-suited to class-based inheritance. Consider the inheritance chain for the window-closing button.

```
Button_close
    Button
        Rect
            Wobj
```

Clearly the window-closing button is a specialized instance of the generic `Button`. Equally clearly, the `Button` is a specialized `Rect` and the `Rect` is one of the objects you need to show on the screen, a specialized window object. At least this part of *JSWindows* fits very

111

well into a class-based OOP inheritance hierarchy. (Not by accident. That's why we chose the project.)

But the question remains, given the material we've covered, do we have a general design approach and how would that approach effect a fresh design for *JSWindows*? We offer some thoughts, especially for those who come from an OOP background.

Use *ex nihilo* Constantly

Creation of objects "out of nothing" is highly recommended. It is a great programming convenience and can lead to very readable code.

Array Literals

We use array literals in *JSWindows* in creating `Wobj`s. Consider Listings 7-1 and 7-2.

Listing 7-1
```
wind = new Window(...
        new Pos_size(100,200, 400,300),...);
// or
wind = new Window(...[100,200, 400,300],...);
```

Listing 7-2
```
... new Window(...
    new Borders(8, 'ridge', 'orange'),...);
// or
... new Window(...[8,'ridge', 'orange'),...);
```

These pairs give the same result. A little extra code in the composition objects' constructors, to let them handle an array argument, makes our lives much easier. (Consider how often you will create an object that you need to display on the screen, in any non-trivial application.)

Styles Objects

We started using a "styles" object as soon as we started creating DOM objects in JavaScript. Listing 7-3 shows a sample styles object.

Listing 7-3

```
var styles = {
    backgroundColor: '#f0f0ff',
    fontSize: '10pt',
    textAlign: 'center'
};
```

When we create a `Wobj` (or any object that inherits from `Wobj`) we permit a `styles` object for those few hundred CSS styles that may be applied. (Yes, there are hundreds.) We've been using this technique for years because it works.

Other Objects

By "other" we specifically mean those properties of `Wobj` and `Wobj`-based objects that attach directly to the DOM object, not to the DOM element's `style` object. Will this `Rect` be the "name" input field? `{innerHTML: 'inupt field here'}` does nicely early in the project.

In idle moments we ask ourselves why *ex nihilo* objects, objects that have no prototype, were first created in languages that used prototypal inheritance. There must be a moral in that story. They are invaluable in class-based inheritance, too.

Use Composition Liberally

Our second principal is to completely agree with the Gang of Four and use composition where it fits. We began the *JSWindows* system by writing the first versions of the `Pos_size` and `Borders` methods. `Wobj` was not written until these were well tested.

We looked at the `Borders` methods in Chapter 2. Here we'll take another look at composition courtesy of the `Pos_size` family.

Original `Pos_size`

`Pos_size` is the "position and size" family. To put an object on the screen you must tell it where it go and how big you want it to be. An early version allowed two optional arguments for `right` and `bottom` positions, when we chose to position that way. More on those in a moment.

Somehow the rich supply of CSS length suffixes never found its way into our code. We've grown fond of 'px' (and have been badly burned trying to work in 'em' and other units). Sometimes we missed '%' but our `styles` objects let us have its functionality when needed.

In addition to letting us specify position and size, the `Pos_size` methods let us specify them our way. Specifically, we seldom found the CSS definitions for size (size of the content area, inside padding and border) to be helpful in screen layout. We wanted size to mean the size within and including the borders. Our `pos_size` objects were never measured any other way. We buried the computations needed to comply with CSS dictates inside the `Pos_size` and `Borders` methods, where we could forget about them.

Mature Pos_size

We were tired of fighting with CSS, trying to position sizing buttons left of the closing button in the top-right corner of a window, when we bit the bullet and wrote our `Pos_size` specification parser, shown in Listing 7-4. It proves that a little bit of regex can go a long way.

Listing 7-4

```
Pos_size.parse_ps = function (spec) {

/*     BOS, opt whitespace
( digits opt(.opt digits) ) | (.digits) )
    opt whitespace
    opt ((+|-)digits)
    opt whitespace
    opt (B|b|C|c)
    opt chars, EOS */

var re = /^\s*((\d+(\.\d*)?)|(\.\d+))\s*((\
+|\-)\d+)?\s*(B|b|C|c)?.*$/;

    spec.replace(',', '.').match(re);
    return {
            ratio: +RegExp.$1,
            offset: +RegExp.$5,
            type:
        (RegExp.$7 === 'C') ||
        (RegExp.$7 === 'c') ? 'C' : 'B'
    };

} // end: Pos_size.parse_ps()
```

The regex is, as always, powerful and unreadable. We try to compensate by having more comment (highlighted) than code when we use regex.

The regex parses position and size specs of the form:

```
'ratio [+|-offset] [B|C]'
```

where `ratio` is a number between 0.0 and 1.0, inclusive,

`offset` is a number of pixels, and

`B` (default) or `C` means relative to Border or Content area.

The `ratio` is the amount of the free space that should be placed on the left (or top) of the element. Free space is the number of pixels between the element's border and the edge of the container's border (`B`) or content area (`C`). 0.0 positions the element at the left (or top); 1.0 positions the element at the right (or bottom). The offset is added to (subtracted from) this position. Once we created the ratio specification we had no more need for the CSS right and bottom specifications. The close button we prefer is two pixels in from the right, two down from the top: `'1.0 -2'`, `'0.0 +2'`. This is, by default, in the window's border. (The regex allows "1" in lieu of "1.0" if you dislike typing.)

Having fought a losing battle with CSS's minimal ability to center an element horizontally, and its total inability to center vertically, we are delighted to be able to achieve either by simply specifying a ratio of `'0.5'`. To center an element, horizontally and vertically, with just `'0.5'`, `'0.5'` is a joy.

Composition and capabilities are similar in that they are shared across families. In *JSWindows* every `Wobj`-based element has a `Pos_size` and a `Borders`. Like objects, they help to reduce a large program into small program pieces. For example, the parser in listing 7-4 is not simple, but it does not interact with other pieces. Its isolation makes it possible to debug, or, if necessary, replace.

Use Capabilities Liberally

Capabilities have proven their value in JavaScript mixins and Java interfaces. The latter originally found their purpose as a way of avoiding multiple inheritance's issues. Like interfaces, capabilities let us escape from complexities such as diamond inheritance hierarchies. Interfaces later became preferred for many reasons, most of which reflect their good fit with many real world objects. Capabilities, which are implemented interfaces (supercharged with some OP), share these benefits.

Some humans are computer programmers. Some humans pilot small planes. Some play tennis. Each of these is a capability which does not depend on the other capabilities. Each capability can be learned (programmed) independently, isolating a piece of the system. Tennis playing does not interact with computer programming. A human could do one or the other, both or neither.

Our *JSWindows* inheritance chains could be eliminated by more aggressive use of capabilities. For example, we could add a capability list parameter to the `Rect` constructor. A `Rect` that implements `Closable` replaces our `Window`. A `Rect` that

implements `Closable` and `Movable` replaces our `Window_M`. A
`Rect` that implements `Closable` and `Button_sizable` does not
even exist in our inheritance hierarchy, although it may be exactly
what is wanted in some situations.

Just as programming objects helps reduce large systems to a set of
smaller, independent subsystems, separating capabilities from objects
further reduces program size.

Use Inheritance Conservatively

Inheritance is useful only when the extending family is a superset of
the extended family. Let's return to our first figure, Figure 4-1.

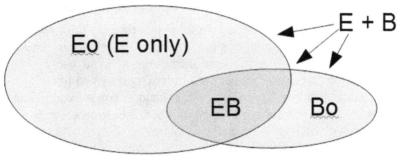

Figure 4-1

Inheritance is a valid model for E and B only when Bo is empty. This
is a very specific, limited situation.

That does not mean, however, that it occurs infrequently. The success
of C++, Java and the rest of the OOP family shows this. It is also
possible, as *JSWindows* shows, to design this relationship (empty Bo)
into a system deliberately. While we don't recommend forcing
systems into an OOP inheritance pattern, we do recommend using
OOP inheritance when that matches the reality a system models.

When we redesign *JSWindows* we will not remove the `Window`, just
because it is a `Rect` with capabilities. A "window" is a well known
user interface component, in systems we all use. As a convenience,
we will adopt the name as a shorthand for a `Rect` fitted out with
common window capabilities. We'll make ours `Closable`,
`Movable`, `Button_sizable` and `Maskable`. This will make it very

easy to create the most common windows. Our main hierarchy will be simplified to:

```
Window
    Wobj
```

We might cut out the `Rect` middle man, but closing and sizing buttons really need an inheritance chain like this:

```
Button_close, Button_sizable
    Button
        Wobj
```

One final note on inheritance. JavaScript inheritance chains, when inheritance is used, should be short. Possibly. This advice is almost universal. If inheritance chains are shortened when you use construction and capabilities and avoid forcing reality to fit inheritance, then we agree. On the other hand, if you are using short chains because JavaScript's prototypal inheritance grows less efficient with each added prototype lookup, we disagree. As *JSWindows* shows, OOP inheritance chains in JavaScript are simple to create and maintain without using chained prototypal lookups. We only use the prototype to store instance methods and never look past the instance's immediate prototype, regardless of the length of the inheritance chain. We see no need for prototype chains. Inheritance chains should be as long as required for the reality you model.

Model reality. JavaScript does not reward you for avoiding OOP inheritance, nor does it penalize you for using OOP inheritance when it provides an apt model. The same is also true of prototypal inheritance. If your reality has objects that inherit from prototype objects, JavaScript will support you.

Summary

OOP inheritance is a technique for creating two families, one extending another. The extending family is a superset of the base family. Prototypal inheritance is a technique for creating a second object based on a prototype object.

Using either type of inheritance, objects commonly have different data properties but share methods with their sibling objects. Using OOP languages, the methods are written in the OOP class. Using JavaScript, the methods may be written in the object prototype.

Using prototypal lookup chains is not efficient in JavaScript. The technique shown in our *JSWindows* demonstration system shows long inheritance chains programmed without prototypal lookup chains. When your software models a system that includes an inheritance chain, long or short, using JavaScript's mixed class-based/prototypal object model lets your code map easily to your reality.

Finally, unlike static OOP languages, JavaScript lets the programmer manipulate objects during execution. Objects may be created *ex nihilo,* from nothing, and object properties may be added and deleted as the program warrants. In JavaScript, the programmer can work with object properties, including their names and values. In OOP, the programmer works only with property values during execution time, a serious limitation.

We also suggest programming with "capabilities," mixins that implement Java interfaces, as one way of taking advantage of JavaScript's object programming to extend the gains made by using software objects.

8 On OOP Principles

(This chapter is directed specifically at an audience well versed in class-based OOP concepts.)

> According to the principles of object-oriented programming, all OOP languages have three traits in common: encapsulation, polymorphism and inheritance.
>
> Subhasis Nayak

The above declaration is typical in discussion of OOP's main principles or concepts. Encapsulation, polymorphism and inheritance have been cited as the "big three" as commonly as any. In Wikipedia's excellent article on OOP, one section is devoted to the foolishness of picking any three characteristics of OOP in this manner (and we agree). But Nayak is correct, if one is looking for the three most commonly cited features.

Ranking OOP Principles

We asked Google for its first 20 entries on "object-oriented principles." From its list we removed duplicates and those sources which did not clearly enumerate principles. We were left with fourteen lists. The principles, in order of frequency of citation, are:

1. Inheritance (12 of 14 cite inheritance)
2. Encapsulation (11)
3. Polymorphism (11)
4. Classes (8)
5. Abstraction (7)
6. Interfaces (5)
7. Composition (3)
8. Cohesion, abstract classes, coupling, messages (2 each)
9. Aggregation, Association, Components, Delegation, Dynamic Dispatch, Events, Modularity, Overloading, Overriding, Packages, Properties, Recursion, Specialization (1 each)

(For the source lists, with principles, see the end of this chapter.)

In this chapter we look carefully at the "big three," and at the other OOP concepts to see how JavaScript's object programming capabilities address the same needs.

Inheritance

Over half this book has been directed specifically at inheritance, class-based and prototypal. (In our survey of OOP concepts, prototypal techniques received exactly zero citations, from which fact the reader is free to draw conclusions.) We feel it unarguable that JavaScript's choice of inheritance types and support for both class-based and prototypal models is generally superior to the class-based languages' support. We move on to the concepts not already discussed.

Encapsulation

An object can "encapsulate" information. One common technique is to provide access to the object's data properties through object methods. In Java, for example, data properties might be declared `private` while reading and writing methods are declared `public`.

This lets an object hide details that are not relevant and expose only information that is needed by the outside. In U.S. life insurance, for example, a customer's "insurable age" means "age at the nearest birthday." (An infant becomes one year old at six months, two years old after 18 months, and so on.) A `public get_age()` method could return the appropriate result, without revealing the details of the computation. If the algorithm for insurable age were to change (due to changes in the law, for example) there is only one routine that needs to be updated. External systems do not access the private properties (such as date of birth).

Access Specifiers

Most class-based OOP languages have keywords that specify access permissions. Java, for example provides `private`, `protected` and `public` as well as default (also called "package private") access. The trend has been to eliminate terminology that suggests these somehow provide data security. They don't. (The choice of the word "protected" was a mistake.)

If Mallory (the security expert's universal bad guy) has access to your system's source code, he will simply change `private` to `public` and then work his mischief. The hope is that your well-intentioned programmers, not Mallory, will work within the object's intended design, accessing properties through appropriate access methods.

JavaScript has no access specifiers. A convention has been adopted, although not universally, that a property name starting with an underscore character is private, not to be accessed. (Methods will provide the needed access to the private properties.) Any such convention requires management support to ensure that it is known and respected throughout an organization. In some environments, this is inadequate.

Closures

The JavaScript solution to provide true access limitation may be to wrap private property values in "closures," bundles of a primary function with other functions and variables. The values of variables in a closure are not accessible except to the functions in the closure.

The mechanics of closures are well covered in other JavaScript literature. They are not, however, a tool for JavaScript beginners. It takes a higher level of JavaScript programming skill to wrap values in closures and to maintain the code that does so. One has to weigh, as always, costs and benefits.

We conclude that other languages are better at encapsulation than JavaScript. If closures are needed they are available, but they are not free.

Polymorphism

There are two good reasons to learn the meaning of polymorphism. First, using such a fancy word in casual conversation makes you sound intelligent. Second, polymorphism provides one of the most useful programming techniques of the object-oriented paradigm.

objects and Java

Morpheus was the God of Dreams, the one with the amazing ability of appearing in dreams of mortals in any form.

god of dreams

Unlike encapsulation, which has a reasonably well-agreed purpose, polymorphism has no single agreed meaning, except that of the word origin. *Poly,* many, and *morph,* from the Greek—as in the god Morpheus—means shape, or form. Commonly used in biology for species with multiple appearances, one dictionary traces the word back to 1839. Unfortunately, the word, in computer science, has itself become polymorphic, supporting many meanings.

One source identifies four types of polymorphism: subtype, parametric, ad-hoc and coercion. We discuss these here.

Subtype Polymorphism

Bill Venners, writing in objects and Java, says polymorphism is the ability to treat an object of any subclass of a base class as if it were an object of the base class. A base class has, therefore, many forms: the base class itself, and any of its subclasses.

(Remember that "subclass" is commonly used to refer to what we call an "extending" class. Also, it is common in writing about "polymorphism" to write about subtype polymorphism, ignoring other types.)

Assume you have a base type, `Animal`, with extending types for `Cats` and `Cows`:

```
cat.speak(); // "Meow, meow"
cow.speak(); // "Moo, moo."
```

The `speak()` method of the `Animal` class returns a result appropriate to the type of animal. We are using `speak()` polymorphically.

There are many ways to achieve this result. The polymorphic method could be defined, in C++, as a virtual method in a virtual base class. It could be defined, in Java, in an interface implemented by the extending classes. In JavaScript, the method my be defined in each extending class's prototype.

The most common example in the literature is the `Shape` class which is extended by classes for `Square`, `Circle`, `Triangle`, and so on. The polymorphic method `area()` is implemented appropriately in the extending classes. See Webopedia for a typical example.

One of the grandest sounding words in object jargon is polymorphism. The essence of polymorphsim is that it allows you to avoid writing an explicit conditional when you have objects whose behavior varies depending on their types.

SourceMaking

This is another example where "polymorphism" clearly means "subtype polymorphism." Your code simply says `object.area()` and the `area()` method appropriate to the object is used. If your application has an array of `Shape` objects, you can compute the total area by looping through them, adding each `Shape`'s `area()` to the total. Without polymorphism, the body of your loop would be a switch with one case for `squares`, another for `circles` and so on.

See these additional links for subtype polymorphism in your favorite language: C++, Java, C#. (The C# docs, from Microsoft, also state, "Polymorphism is often referred to as the third pillar of object-oriented programming, after encapsulation and inheritance." There is no shortage of agreement among those who choose a "big three" that this is one of them.

While most C++-based discussion focuses on extending base classes, often virtual base classes, Java interfaces are discussed for that language (and sometimes discussed with considerable wit). One college course stresses the interface's ability to avoid implementation details.

Parametric Polymorphism

Although there is disagreement about the implementations, there is no disagreement about the terminology when we get to "parametric polymorphism."

In C++, templates can be written that describe methods that may be applied to multiple underlying types.

In Java, a similar mechanism allows for "generic" programming. You can provide functions that apply to Lists, and apply these, polymorphically, to ArrayLists and all other Java list types.

Other languages, such as C#, provide similar functionality although in different ways.

In these examples, each language supports parametric polymorphism as an advanced capability, where it will be seen less commonly than subtype polymorphism.

Ad-hoc and Other Polymorphism

Forms of polymorphism that go beyond subtype and parametric are often called "ad-hoc" polymorphism. You should be aware that there is widespread disagreement about what to name these types of polymorphism, and even whether they actually should be called polymorphism.

A function that works over many different types of arguments may be called polymorphic, as this Haskell source asserts.

Operators that are overloaded to support multiple operand types may be called polymorphic, as this C++ source asserts.

Functions that have different signatures (parameter lists) may be called polymorphic, as this Java source asserts.

Our original list of polymorphism types included "coercion," by which the author specifically referred to Java casts. To think about this, go back to first principles. If a method adds a `foo` and a `bar` property it will return a result (not guaranteed to be sensible, but at least guaranteed to be a result) when applied to any object that has a `foo` and `bar` property that can be added. (Assume that "added" means "can be used on opposite sides of a plus operator.")

If a base class has a `foo` and a `bar` property, any extending class will also have those properties and can also provide a result for any function that uses those properties. However, there is no law that says our base and extending classes are the only ones that might have `foo` and `bar` properties. Myriad, seemingly unrelated, classes may have these properties. A function that adds `foo` and `bar` will produce a result as long as its object has `foo` and `bar`. Therefore this function can be applied to any object with `foo` and `bar` properties. Some will call this polymorphic.

In Java, the compiler happily accepts an extending type when a base type is required. By using a cast, the programmer tells the compiler, "use this type, too. I know what I'm doing. Trust me." As in other areas of life such trust is sometimes justified. Using functions of mismatched types via casting may be called polymorphism. One source called it coercion polymorphism.

JavaScript and Polymorphism

Now that we agree on what polymorphism is (or at least can share an enumeration of some of the things that might be called polymorphic) we can look at how JavaScript enjoys its benefits. In a word, "fully."

When speaking of subtype polymorphism, no language has a richer set of choices for making cows say "Moo" while cats say "meow." (Or for computing the areas of Shapes, if you prefer.)

Place a generic function in the base class prototype. If there is no more sensible default, have the base class method return undefined. (Or, save yourself the trouble. If there is no base function, JavaScript's prototype chain lookups will return undefined on their own.)

Override the base method with more specific methods in each extending class's prototype. Or let the base class return an instance's saying property. If Fish have nothing to say:

```
Fish.prototype.saying = function() {
        return ''; }
```

If Worms have a similar vocabulary:

```
Worm.prototype.saying = Fish.prototype.saying;
```

(You will not do this if there is even a remote possibility that fish and worms might have different sayings, of course. It might be better to give them separate methods even at the risk of repeating yourself.)

Classes, Abstraction and Interfaces

For the "big three" object concepts, we decidedly prefer JavaScript's inheritance, as it lets you choose between class-based and prototypal. We prefer class-based access specifiers for enforcing encapsulation. (They may not be better, but they are easier.) And we love JavaScript's flexibility when it comes to polymorphism's main form. Now we look at the second trio of commonly cited object concepts.

Classes

Before we start on classes, note again that "objects" (or "instances") were discarded when our source lists included them. Calling "objects" one of the most important concepts in programming with objects seemed redundant. Classes, however, were not redundant.

Unfortunately, none of the eight lists that included classes even mentioned the fact that some languages have objects, but do not have classes. A reader would get the impression that classes are somehow necessary to programming with objects. Clearly, as JavaScript shows, you can dispense with the classes but retain the objects, so the rest of the discussion is highly suspect, to say the least.

On the other hand, this book has gone to some length to explain how JavaScript's constructors, including their attached properties, are functionally equivalent to the class-based languages' classes. The question isn't whether JavaScript has classes; the question is whether you choose to use the word "class" in two slightly different ways, one of which is broad enough to cover JavaScript constructors.

Clearly, JavaScript has class functionality. We will all be broad minded about letting each other choose word meanings. As engineers, we'll use JavaScript's constructors to create objects, JavaScript's `constructor.prototype` to store method code, and so on.

Abstraction

Seven of our fourteen lists include abstraction. What do they mean?

The term "abastraction" is commonly applied during the design phase when base classes are being discussed. It refers to the simplification process that goes from specifics toward fundamental class definitions.

Our business has "customers." What do we mean by that? What are the fundamental principles of customers? A law office serving customers will have a deeper understanding of the individuals involved than will, for instance, a fast-food restaurant. To the former, a customer has phone number(s), email address(es) and so on. To the latter, the customer's individual data is irrelevant.

A JavaScripter should avoid abstraction, not because it is an unimportant concept, but because a semi-prototypal language has no use for long inheritance chains, and therefore no use for the kind of deep thinking involved in designing class hierarchies.

Maybe. Designing with inheritance as a key tool, in class-based languages, is a well-understood topic. C++ has been with us for thirty years as this is written. JavaScript's "capabilities" are mere babies by comparison. What important principles will emerge as JavaScript-specific designs grow up? There may be another way of looking at abstraction.

Interfaces

Java's interfaces were originally presented as a poor man's alternative to multiple inheritance. Today they are vastly more important, and multiple inheritance is almost forgotten. (Interfaces were cited by five of our fourteen lists. Multiple inheritance: zero.)

The classic Gang of Four book tells us to code to interfaces, not implementations. In Java, the interface is a rigorous description of the properties, sometimes data and almost always methods, that are available outside an object. An implementation is a specific class that implements the interface. The GoF advice, if followed, has us using the interface in the way it was designed, not the way it was implemented.

A specific class may be very badly written. It might be large, slow and/or buggy. If we code to the interface, the day will come when someone rewrites the class so that it is small, fast and elegant. Our code, if it was written to the interface, is unchanged.

(Well, that's the theory. In fact, the programmer who discovers the small, fast, elegant core will probably also discover that the interface needs some tweaking, too. Those changes are still likely to be much easier for us if we program to the interface.)

Interfaces, in JavaScript, are likely to exists as documentation, not code. Good documentation is worth its weight in gold, in JavaScript, or class-based code. Documenting the API before writing code is a good idea in any language.

Other OOP Principles

Of the remaining principles in our lists, composition gets the most citations (3). It has already received two major citations in this book.

One more citation: the GoF tell us to prefer composition over inheritance. That is one of their two major non-pattern recommendations.

Of the remaining principles in the two citation group, messaging deserves some comment. Messaging (or message passing) was a key feature of the Smalltalk object system. It simply did not catch on. (The jargon deteriorated alarmingly. At its worst, calling functions became a form of "message passing.") Most OOP practitioners seem to live happily without Smalltalk's messages.

In the one-citation category we find association and aggregation. These are specific types of composition. (Perhaps they should be added to composition's total.) If they help you prefer composition over inheritance, use them.

Several of the remaining one-citation principles owe their entire support to the Wikipedia article. Sorry to say, this article is not very good at picking the leading principles of object-oriented programming. A thorough edit would help.

Summary

With a single exception, encapsulation, JavaScript excels at the principles said to underlie object-oriented programming. Do you suppose that giving an object a property named "private" and attaching any private values to it would help? Some experimenting along these lines seems in order.

Surveyed Pages

1) Dynamic dispatch, Encapsulation, Subtype polymorphism, Inheritance (delegation), Open recursion. Also Classes, Methods, Message passing, Abstraction. https://en.wikipedia.org/wiki/Object-oriented_programming

2) Abstraction, Specialization, Encapsulation, Inheritance, Polymorphism http://www.jamesbooth.com/OOPBasics.htm

3) Encapsulation, Abstraction, Inheritance, Polymorphism
http://codebetter.com/raymondlewallen/2005/07/19/4-major-principles-of-object-oriented-programming/

4) Class Members, Inheritance, Interfaces, Encapsulation, Polymorphism
http://help.adobe.com/en_US/AS2LCR/Flash_10.0/help.html?content=00000159.html

5) Data Abstraction, Encapsulation, Message, Method, Class, Inheritance, Late binding polymorphism, Abstract classes, Interface, Delegation, Generic classes and Interfaces
http://catdir.loc.gov/catdir/samples/cam032/99087328.pdf

6) Class, Inheritance, Interface, Package
http://docs.oracle.com/javase/tutorial/java/concepts/

7) Class, Encapsulation, Association, Aggregation and Composition, Abstraction and Generalization, Abstract Class, Interface, Inheritance, Polymorphism, Overloading and Overriding
http://www.codeproject.com/Articles/22769/Introduction-to-Object-Oriented-Programming-Concep

8) Classes, Abstraction
http://www.csee.wvu.edu/~ammar/cpp/cpp.html

9) Inheritance, Abstraction, Encapsulation, Polymorphism, Cohesion and Coupling http://www.slideshare.net/TelerikAcademy/25-object-oriented-programming-principles-c-fundamentals

10) "According to the principles of object-oriented programming, all OOP languages have three traits in common: encapsulation, polymorphism and inheritance."
http://www.slideshare.net/snykmcajob/oops-and-c-fundamentals

11) Class, Abstraction, Polymorphism, Inheritance, Encapsulation, Composition, Cohesion, Coupling, Interface
http://javarevisited.blogspot.com/2010/10/fundamentals-of-object-oriented.html

12) Modularity, Encapsulation, Reuse (Composition, Inheritance)
http://javarevisited.blogspot.com/2010/10/fundamentals-of-object-oriented.html

13) Classes, Polymorphism, Components
http://zone.ni.com/devzone/cda/ph/p/id/45

14) Properties, Methods, Events, Subclassing (Inheritance),
Polymorphism, encapsulation
http://www.dfpug.com/loseblattsammlung/migration/whitepapers/Fu
ndOOP.htm

9 On Constructors

Constructor Magic

Now we look at the "magic" in the constructor. By "magic" we mean to criticize, not praise, JavaScript. Code that is free from magic is code that is easy to read, and therefore to maintain.

When we say "constructor", bear in mind that a function is not a constructor because it starts with a capital letter. It is a constructor because it is used after the `new` operator, which is where we can start.

The new Operator

The new operator is privileged. It looks at the argument to its right (the constructor function) and dives into its internals to make certain "improvements." Here we'll look closely at these improvements.

The this Parameter

In general, you cannot explain JavaScript's uses of this with simple, regular rules. These remarks refer to the this created by new.

First, the new operator creates a new, empty object that will be passed to the constructor as the this parameter. Listing 9-1 is a sample Dog constructor.

Listing 9-1

```
function Dog(name, breed) {
    this.name = name;
    this.breed = breed;
}
```

When used after the new operator, this is a reference to the initially empty object passed to the constructor.

A common JavaScript pattern, that helps readability, is the "Single this" pattern. It states that this should appear no more than once in any function and its single appearance should be at the top, where a new, meaningful name is assigned. Using the "Single this" pattern, the above function would be written as Listing 9-2 shows:

Listing 9-2

```
function Dog(name, breed) {
    var new_dog = this;

    new_dog.name = name;
    new_dog.breed = breed;
}
```

The this parameter is also special in that you can assign properties to it, but you cannot change its value (the object that new assumes is being fitted out with properties). You cannot assign to it even if you have given it a nice, meaningful name.

The `constructor.prototype`

The `new` operator relies on the fact that the constructor function (actually, every function, because any function might be used as a constructor) has a `prototype` property. In our example, that is `Dog.prototype`. JavaScript functions are objects and you can attach properties to them, just as you can with any other objects. (Functions that are no less capable than other objects are often called "first-class" functions. These are essential for "functional programming," as in the Scheme dialect of Lisp, one of JavaScript's other forebears.)

Crockford says (*The Good Parts,* p. 47) "The new function object is given a prototype property whose value is an object containing a constructor property whose value is the new function object." Crockford's writing can be dense. Let's take this one step at a time. The result is simple.

"The new function object ..."} First, let's create a new function object (functions are a type of object).

```
function Dog(name, breed) { ... }
```

If you prefer, we could assign a reference to an anonymous function to a variable:

```
var Dog = function (name, breed) { ... }
```

"... is given a prototype property..." Let's give our new function object a property named "prototype":

```
Dog.prototype = ... ;
```

"... whose value is an object ..." That property named "prototype" is, to be precise, a reference to an object. Let's assign an object literal.

```
Dog.prototype = {...};
```

"... containing a constructor property ..." That object literal needs a property named "constructor".

```
Dog.prototype = {constructor: ...};
```

"... whose value is the new function object." Well, now we've come full circle. Remember the new function object? That was `Dog`. So the value of our property is, to be exact, a reference to the function object:

```
Dog.prototype = {constructor: Dog};
```

When you create a function, any function (let's try another for cat lovers) JavaScript gives it a property named "prototype" which refers to an object. Then JavaScript gives that object a single property, named "constructor" and it assigns a reference to the function as the value of that property.

```
Cat.prototype = {constructor: Cat};
```

The `new` operator relies on the function having a property that is an object named "prototype" and the fact that this object has a property named "constructor" whose value is a reference to the function. To give credit (or blame) where it is due, this magic is performed by the `Function` constructor.

The "[[prototype]]" Property

Next we come to "[[prototype]]" which you see immediately is a string in quotes, not something highlighted as actual code. This is because "[[prototype]]" is the name the JavaScript standards (ECMAScript) give to a property internal to the object being created in a constructor. (We said above that `new` created an empty object. Before the object was handed to the constructor, it was given this ghostly property. The value of "[[prototype]]" is a reference to the `prototype` property of the constructor function, in our example, a reference to `Dog.prototype`.

You cannot read nor write the "[[prototype]]" nor even follow the reference. In Firefox's JavaScript, and in the latest versions of the ECMAScript standards, "[[prototype]]" is also the `__proto__` property of the object instance. (You might want to forget that `__proto__` exists until it is available in all major browsers.)

The Prototype's Prototype

The value assigned to "[[prototype]]" is a reference to the constructor's property named "prototype". (Remember, this property —Dog.prototype, for example—is an object.) In our example, this would be:

```
Dog.prototype.constructor = Dog;
```

(Just what Crockford said.)

That assigns a reference to the constructor function to the constructor's prototype property, where it can be accessed as if it were an instance property.

```
alert(lassie.constructor); // Dog reference
```

Why? Again, that's a prototype lookup. A prototype lookup is actually a lookup in the "[[prototype]]" property's value. For an object created by Dog, that will be a lookup in the Dog.prototype object. Lassie has no property named "constructor" so JavaScript looks in her prototype. Lassie's constructor function is Dog, and her prototype is the object Dog.prototype. The value of that object's "constructor" property is a reference to the Dog function, from which Lassie was constructed.

"[[prototype]]" Implies

It is hard to overestimate the importance of "[[prototype]]". It refers to a property of the constructor. That implies that every object created by the constructor shares the same "[[prototype]]" property. Stop and think slowly. Every member of the Dog family, in prototypal terms, "inherits" from Dog.prototype.

Unlike true prototypal inheritance, where one object inherits from a prototype object, in JavaScript every member of the family inherits from Dog.prototype. Were we not avoiding the word "class" because of its ambiguities, we would say that the class inherits from the object prototype. This means that JavaScript, in spite of the use of the name "prototype," is at the most fundamental level closer to class-based inheritance than to prototypal inheritance.

Note that in class-based OOP, the class software creates the properties of each instance one at a time. With a JavaScript object assigned as the prototype, it is the prototype object to which the properties are assigned, one at a time, to define properties of the family. You will see numerous assignments to `xxx.prototype` (where `xxx` is a reference to a constructor) if you look at the *JSWindows* software.

The Constructor Returns `this`

The final magic is that the constructor, without a return statement, works as if it ended with a line that says:

```
return this;
```

In practice, it's likely that the `new` operator retains a reference to the object it creates and passes to the constructor as `this`. JavaScript constructors should not have explicit `return` statements. (Some do use explicit returns so that a single function can be used as a constructor, sometimes, and as a plain function, other times. This is a prescription for unreadable code.)

With this much magic, a summary is in order.

The "Magic" Summarized

The `new` operator appears to be a unary operator, except that it opens the constructor function on its right and makes some invisible modifications. The first of these is to add an invisible parameter named `this`, a reference to the object being created.

The constructor function (call it `cfunc`), courtesy of the `Function` constructor, has a property named "prototype." The value of this property is an object that has just one property named "constructor." `prototype.constructor` holds a reference to the constructor function, `cfunc`. The `new` operator assigns a reference to the constructor's "prototype" object property as the value of a ghostly (no reading or writing allowed) property referred to as "[[prototype]]".

The value of "[[prototype]]" in the object called `this` in the `Dog` constructor is set to `Dog.prototype`. The value of `Dog.prototype.constructor` is `Dog`.

JavaScript, when it is asked for a property of an instance of `Dog` that is not a property of the instance will look in the instance's prototype (referred to as "[[prototype]]" and set to be `Dog.prototype`. If you ask for a `Dog` instance's "constructor" property and there is no property of that name in the instance, JavaScript will look for it in the prototype of the instance, `Dog.prototype`, where it will find a property named "constructor" and return the value. That value is `Dog` (more precisely, a reference to the `Dog` function object).

Every member of the `Dog` family is created by the `Dog` constructor. That means that every `Dog` object has `Dog.prototype` as its prototype. A single object is the prototype for the entire family (class) of `Dog`s. This is very like an entire family in the class-based OOP model sharing the OOP class software.

Finally, the `new` operator retains a reference to the object that it passed to the constructor as `this`, and behaves as if the constructor ended with the statement `return this;`, passing the `this` reference on to the operator on its left.

Constructors Are Not for Inheritance

At first look, the task seems simple. To create an instance of E that extends B, start the E constructor by creating an instance of B. Consider the example in Listing 9-3.

Listing 9-3

```
function E() {

    this = new B();
ABOVE IS AN ERROR!

    new_e.more_props = more_values;
    … // other E properties here
}
```

Because of the "magic" of JavaScript constructors they are not suitable for extending families. E cannot simply embed a call to the B constructor in its own constructor.

You might want to start as shown above, but it is specifically prohibited. You cannot assign to `this` in a constructor. Suppose you could write the code in Listing 9-3. What would the value of "[[prototype]]" be when you create an instance of E?

```
var an_e = new E();
```

Should the value of "[[prototype]]" be `E.prototype`? That is the rule. The "[[prototype]]" is the prototype property of the constructor function. But why not `B.prototype`? Follow the same rule for the line inside E:

```
    this = new B();
```

Clearly `this`'s "[[prototype]]" is `B.prototype`! JavaScript avoids this ambiguity by making assignment to `this` illegal in constructors.

Giving the object referenced by `this` a meaningful name, such as new_e, does not let you get around the rule. If you assign a reference to the `this` object to new_e, then write `new_e = new B();` you no longer have a reference to the `this` object in new_e.

Notes

References, as in a bibliography, should be online. (At least until you can place your mouse on a printed page and click, online will be preferred.)

The gateway to the online portion of this book is http://www.martinrinehart.com/frontend-engineering/knowits/op/knowits-op.html.

The gateway page provides links to references.

Defined Terms

Often the most controversial portion of an analysis is the definitions. We have attempted to use terms that have (more or less) common definitions and avoid terms that are ambiguous (e.g., polymorphism). Wikipedia is particularly valuable in having a community editing process that often achieves consensus on definitions. We also check other sources, however. Our defined terms and their references include:

Object-oriented programming Oop-W, Oop-1-5

Prototype-based programming Prtp-W, Prtp-1-5

Classes Clss-W, Clss-1-6

Instances (objects) Inst-W, Inst-1-4

Methods Mthd-W, Mthd-1-4

Inheritance Inhr-W, Inhr-1-6

Composition Cmp-W, Cmp-1-4

(A second dash, as in Oop-1-5, denotes the full range: Oop-1, Oop-2, ..., Oop-5.)

Support for Selected Statements

"Today even 50-year old languages (Basic, Cobol, Fortran) have adopted objects." `Oop-3`, `Inhr-4`, `Clss-6`, `Mthd-4`

"Other languages, such as Java (1995) adopted the C++ object model." `Clss-1-6`, particularly `Clss-2`

"By contrast, the "prototypal" object paradigm does not use classes. The programmer creates a prototype object and other objects are then copied from the prototype." `Prtp1-4`

"An object is a collection of properties (often a set, but "set" has a mathematical meaning we do not want here). Properties are named values." `Inst-1-4`

"Objects also are permitted direct access to a collection of functions (commonly called "instance methods") that are part of the class (in class-based languages) or the prototype (in JavaScript)." `Inst-3`, `Mthd-1-4`, `Prtp-1`, `Prtp-2`, `Prtp-4`

> "In OOP, a class is the software that creates and supports a set of objects, including the constructor and methods that instances of the class can perform. A class may also have methods and data of its own ("class statics", in Java)." `Clss-1-6`

'In class-based OOP, when Bo is empty we say that E "extends" B, or E "inherits from" B.' `Inhr-2-6`.

[In prototypal inheritance] "Objects inherit directly from each other. The base object is called the "prototype" of the inheriting object. " `Prtp-1-4`

"If an object includes another type of object as a property, it is using composition." `Inhr-1-2`, but see `Inhr-3` and `Inhr-4` for qualifiers.

"[JavaScript] also lets you create an object *ex nihilo* (from nothing)." `Prtp-2`

"We are not endorsing inheritance-based architecture;" `Inhr-1`

'We extend interfaces to "capabilities" which borrow from and extend both Java's interfaces and JavaScript's "mixins."' `Trts-W`,